The Soul-Searcher's Guide to the Galaxy

The Soul-Searcher's Guide to the Galaxy

*Figuring out life's challenges
from housework
to sex
to global warming*

Douglas Todd

Self-Counsel Press
(a division of)
International Self-Counsel Press Ltd.
Canada   U.S.A.

Printed in Canada

First edition: February, 1994

Canadian Cataloguing in Publication Data

Todd, Douglas, 1953–
    The soul-searcher's guide to the galaxy

    (Self-counsel series)
    ISBN 0-88908-770-9

    1. Ethics. I. Title II. Series.
    BJ1012.T62 1994   170   C94-910003-X

Self-Counsel Press
(a division of)
International Self-Counsel Press Ltd.

Head and Editorial Office	*U.S. Address*
1481 Charlotte Road	1704 N. State Street
North Vancouver, British Columbia	Bellingham, Washington
V7J 1H1	98225

Contents

Acknowledgments

To my mother, uncle, and brother, who taught me the world can be a better place.

To my wife, whose instinct for doing the right thing balances my less-than-perfect pragmatism.

To my three young sons, who don't realize they convinced me how important it is to write about values.

To my friends and teachers, who are unwilling to give up, or give in, to cynicism.

To Ruth Wilson of Self-Counsel Press, whose enthusiasm and skill made this project happen.

Finally, to *The Vancouver Sun*, whose editors supported my efforts to make ethics accessible to a wide audience. This book grew out of work begun at the *Sun*. Editor-in-Chief Ian Haysom, in more ways than one, made it possible.

Introduction
The ethics explosion

If your morals make you weary, depend upon it they are wrong.

Robert Louis Stevenson

✦ ✦ ✦ ✦ ✦

From world leaders to TV preachers, from fast-rolling financiers to big-city judges, scandal has been breaking out in high places. In the home, people have been mistrusting their spouses and fudging their taxes. In schools, students cheat on exams. In business, people betray a friend to win a job or contract. In sports, adults and kids do whatever they can to win. Too many people seem to think anything goes — as long as they don't get caught.

It's enough to throw you into depression.

This book is designed to help you deal with the gnawing worry that accepted standards of behavior no longer exist in North America — and that the shifty are being rewarded. It will lead you through the fog shrouding some of life's most common, and most touchy, ethical dilemmas. However, it avoids being doctrinaire; it's not meant to induce clammy feelings of guilt. With a little luck, it may even entertain you.

After an era of acquisition, author Tom Wolfe's prediction that the 1990s will be the decade we talk about values is turning out to be accurate. We're struggling again, as filmmaker Spike Lee put it, over how to do the right thing.

The new passion for ethics has been fueled by baby boomers — and others — who are growing troubled about the kind of world they're passing on to their children. Eighty percent of North Americans now believe morals and ethics should be taught in schools. Researchers say that a letdown in moral values is now considered the number-one problem facing the country.

An ethics explosion has been reverberating from bedrooms to operating rooms, classrooms to boardrooms. The trend-spotting book, *Megatrends 2000*, by John Naisbitt, says more than 6,000 North American schools now offer ethics programs, hundreds of business ethics courses have popped up in colleges and universities, and most hospitals have established ethics committees. Lawyers, engineers, journalists, and doctors are hammering out codes of conduct. The board game, Scruples, is a bestseller, and radio shows have been developed around ethical quizzes. People are investing billions of dollars in ethical mutual funds.

But how do we handle those troublesome ethical hassles we run into every day? We all know we're not supposed to lie, cheat, and steal, yet sometimes that's easier said than done. And many of us are overwhelmed by tough choices involving sex, competition, business, charity, housework, animal rights, abortion, ambition, civil disobedience, the environment, political correctness, pride, anger, health care, conflict of interest, euthanasia, war, ecology, and more.

This book avoids bashing you with a list of shall-nots as it explores these issues. Instead, it tries to help you understand them more deeply. It begins in Part 1 with ethical challenges we run into in the intimacy of our home — where elusively simple things like divvying up housework can drive us to distraction. Part 2 looks at how to interact with your community in a more fulfilling way. In Part 3, you'll find guidance to the rough-and-tumble world of the workplace where money is supposed to rule. The last section of the book, Part 4, explores global issues, such as ecology and war.

For a bit of meaningful fun, each chapter has a quiz-like introduction to get you mulling the kind of choice you'd make in a bind. Many questions don't have straightforward right-or-wrong answers. By the time you finish each chapter, however, you will develop a clearer view of your ethical position — on anything from handling feelings of envy to deciding how much meat you want to eat. Each chapter ends with questions to help you explore your own attitudes and focus your views. The questions are also good for sparking group discussion.

The goal of this book is to empower you by assisting you in figuring out where you stand. It will help you feel better about the hard choices you have to make each day.

May it help you live with integrity.✦

Part 1
Home is where the action is

The strength of a nation is derived from the integrity of its homes.

Confucius

✦ ✦ ✦ ✦ ✦

Ethical challenges invade the most intimate aspects of our lives: from our sexual desires to figuring out whose turn it is to take out the garbage.

At home, every move you make — the food you eat, the way you show you're upset — affects someone else. It's a marvel we make it through the day. It isn't easy to hammer out domestic justice, to act with integrity with those we love, to make sense of life, death, and sex, to forge relationships rather than rip them apart.✦

1. Going crazy over housework

Q: Guests are coming for dinner. You agreed to cook the meal in exchange for your house mate cleaning the home. But your house mate, who doesn't seem to notice when you do chores, is once again late arriving from work. Do you clean up, or leave your home untidy for the guests?

✦ ✦ ✦ ✦ ✦

If you've never had an argument over whose turn it is to wash a stack of dishes, chances are you're either a household despot, a saint, or a reasonable facsimile of a doormat.

Who hasn't felt taken for granted after finishing an unappreciated chore? Since caring for a household is so mundane and inescapable — so daily — it's become the focus of some of our most explosive ethical clashes.

Cooking dinner, taking out garbage, raking leaves, changing diapers, vacuuming the living room, cleaning up toys, repairing a leaky tap, washing windows, putting in eight to 10 hours a day to earn money. It goes on and on and on.

In the past two decades, with men's consciences pricked by the women's movement, and economic pressures forcing most females into the workplace, most of us have had to ponder how to bring justice to our changing homes. And unlike torturously complicated issues like abortion and euthanasia where theoretical debates can rage on inconclusively, nearly everyone believes domestic justice means equality.

The trick is putting that simple, noble theory into practice. In the past few hundred years, with men working outside the home earning the money and, therefore, the prestige, women's work around the home has been devalued, says Peter Danielson of the Centre for Professional and Applied Ethics. Nowadays, however, declining living standards have made it necessary, in many cases, for both male and female to venture outside the home to earn wages equivalent to those that a man used to bring in on his own. Women, in particular, are putting in two shifts a day — at the job and at home. Exceptions exist, but men, in general, aren't quite doing their bit.

Pick your statistic:

- Only 20% of men share housework equally, according to one study.

- About 70% of men do more than a third of the housework, but less than half, and 10% do less than a third.

- Men began doing more housework in the past decade — roughly 10 hours a week of cleaning, cooking, and repairs, according to a 1985 study by *American Demographics* magazine. But women work about 20 hours a week at housework.

- Over a year, the average woman works a full month of 24-hour days more than a man.

- Of 600 couples recently divorced, the second most common reason women cited for ending the marriage was their husbands' "neglect of home or children."

Despite women's liberation, social convention still puts the onus on women to take care of housekeeping and children, Danielson says. "A woman gets blamed for a messy house, even if a man caused it."

Although women have been the big losers when it comes to workloads in the eighties and nineties, men have lost too. It's not particularly justified, but many men feel resentful they can no longer return from work to relax over dinner in a clean home. Everyone seems exhausted.

"I think it's the disease of the age. People are working themselves to death," says Bonnelle Strickling, an ethics specialist who is also a psychologist. "It's not just greed. The nature of people's jobs seems to require them to work too hard. There's very little left for the pleasures of life."

The home is being squeezed by powerful social pressures. Parents, in particular, are under tremendous stress. At a societal level, say the ethicists, we could be considering helping out beleaguered parents by offering more generous maternity and paternity leaves, increasing flex-time opportunities at work, making it easier for people to share jobs, promoting pay equity for women, making child care more affordable, helping out single mothers, and forcing divorced men to make child-support payments.

Some of these are not simple proposals, however, either ethically or financially. Beyond fundamentally changing society, the first thing people should do about housework, say Strickling and Danielson, is discuss it.

"Housework needs a Dr. Ruth," says Danielson, referring to the famous therapist who hosts TV talk-shows where people talk honestly and openly about sex. Consciousness about housework needs to be raised.

Live-in mates should realize there are several major reasons to share responsibility for the household. On the dark side, no one person should have to put up with all the boredom, endless repetition, and potentially stupefying drudgery of housework. "The dust bunnies just never finish," says Strickling.

On the bright side, taking care of a household can be good for the soul. "It's bad for you psychologically if you don't deal with things at the level of cooking and gardening and cleaning. You lose touch with reality," says Strickling. Housework and child care foster a nurturing approach to life.

Toiling at a money-making job should be considered part of caring for a household, say the ethicists. But even in a traditional home, where the husband goes out to a job and the woman stays home, the man should take some responsibility for children and chores. Obviously, a man who doesn't meet some of the everyday demands of child-raising is shirking his role as guardian and won't connect with his children, says Danielson. And a traditional husband who avoids all housework will have no appreciation for those who do.

Just as every citizen has a duty to be informed about civic affairs, Danielson says every member of a household has an obligation to do some housework. Though there's no crystal-clear way to fairly divvy up household commitments, it must be tried. When Strickling lived in a communal house with another woman and two men, they held a meeting at which each person revealed the chores they enjoyed, tolerated, and hated. "We tried to maximize the activities we liked the most." When it came to a task everyone disliked, such as washing dishes and vacuuming the stairs, the foursome devised a rigidly equitable schedule.

Although excessive squalor is probably not too good for anyone, Strickling says chronically tired couples who both work outside the home can choose to lower their cleaning standards. "It sounds trite, but you have to set your priorities," says Strickling. "I personally find it a struggle to take care of my house, my self, get a rest and spend time with people I love. That has to do with values. It's about asking what's worth living for."

It's a delicate issue, but exhausted householders could hire outside people to do some child care or housecleaning. The main danger of hiring out, Strickling says, is it can lead to parents losing touch with their children. It can also promote the already-strong belief that some people are too good for child care or housework; it's only fit for women, young people, or the lower classes. On the other hand, Strickling says, "If you don't think someone who cleans the house is inferior, why put somebody out of work? It's your attitude that can be exploitive. You just shouldn't treat a cleaning person like a thing."

Finally, after trying to equitably balance household responsibilities, it's crucial to show you appreciate it when someone else repairs a door-lock or tidies a playroom. "It's part of respecting the other person," says Strickling. "Most people would rather do anything than housework. Not only do we have to say thanks for housework, we have to attend to it. We have to say to the other person: 'That's a really good job.'"✦

Question box

1. Where you live, do men or women do the most housework?

2. In an ideal world, do you think it would be best if you never had to do housework?

3. What are some fair ways you could reduce fighting over who cleans up, does dishes, and maintains the yard?

2. Sexual tension

Q: As far as you're concerned, your partner does not like sex enough. You meet someone who does. Do you end the old relationship and start a new one?

✦ ✦ ✦ ✦ ✦

Free love. Contraception. Sex for pleasure. Premarital sex. Open marriage. Gay relationships. Serial monogamy.

The sexual revolution that began in the sixties turned our bedrooms upside down and inside out — testing traditional sexual mores that restricted sex to procreation and that banned birth control, homosexuality, and sex outside marriage.

What went on behind closed doors underwent detailed study. The revolution won some battles: more than 80% of Americans and Canadians now approve of premarital sex, according to sociologists. But fewer and fewer people, only about 20%, say extramarital sex is okay.

Sex dominates our thoughts more urgently than any other single interest, say psychologists. Sex can be among humans' most powerful means of communication, laced with terror or ecstasy. But which kind of sexual relationship is right, and which is wrong?

Despite a lot of talk of sexual freedom, fidelity is still a big issue. Sexual commitment falls into three basic forms in the 1990s: life-long monogamy, serial monogamy (one partner at a time for indefinite periods), and open relationships (partners agree they're free to have sex with others).

The only form of sexual commitment that's ethical to conservatives such as philosopher Wesley Cragg is life-long monogamy: most commonly practiced as marriage. The person who wants sex without marriage puts self-interest first, says Cragg, author of *Contemporary Moral Issues*. "The problem with sex outside a life-long commitment is it says to the partner: 'I'm prepared to live with you until it becomes inconvenient to me, or the moment I can find more satisfaction from another person, this relationship is over.'"

The 18th century German philosopher, Immanuel Kant, said humans should treat other humans as "ends, rather than means." And Cragg believes sex outside marriage involves using others merely as a means, "a useful instrument," for one's own pleasure. "Sex outside marriage fails to recognize the bonding of sexual intercourse," says Cragg. "Sexuality generates affection. It exposes the partner to human grief. The person who believes in serial monogamy says: 'I will stay with you only so long as I love you.' It's a contractual view of human relationships, rather than a commitment."

But a nurse who teaches about sexuality in schools across North America challenges Cragg's traditional approach to sexuality. She recommends we avoid being dogmatic about the imperfect world of human sexual interaction. "It's unethical to be judgmental about other relationships," says Meg Hickling. "Marriage is wonderful — if you can do it."

People like Cragg, who condemn pre-marital sex and idolize marriage, drop guilt and a sense of inadequacy on those who are single, says Hickling. Honest serial monogamy can be ethical. Although many still think sex is dirty, Hickling says there is nothing inherently wrong with sex for pleasure.

Sexual conduct should be guided by two principles, says Hickling: consent and maturity. "If two people can consent freely to a sexual relationship, I don't see why that would be unethical. As long as they stick to their agreement. How can an outsider say someone is being used in a sexual relationship, even a recreational one, if that person doesn't feel used?" Hickling defines mature sex as that meant for both oneself and the other (and adds that it's possible among gay couples).

Immature sex occurs when partners feel they have no choice. If a person says yes to sex because she is dependent financially or emotionally, or fears she will be judged harshly for failing married life, she allows herself to be exploited. Children also suffer in floundering marriages that are blindly maintained. Although she recognizes children (and grand-parents) get hurt when a couple splits, she's seen many women in counselling who feel they are not free to divorce alcoholic, abusive, adulterous, or secretly homosexual men because they feel they must "protect" the children.

When it comes to the loosest form of commitment — so-called open relationships — noted philosopher Earle Winkler says ethics are still possible. But Winkler, who took part in the sexually experimental 1960s, agrees with Hickling that open relationships just don't seem to work. The couple who wrote the book, *Open Marriage*, in the early 1970s, later recanted. They concluded open marriage is impossible, especially when kids are involved.

Most of those practicing open sexuality eventually want a primary relationship, a main squeeze, a co-vivant, a signif-icant other. Multiple partners "undermine intimacy and trust," Winkler says. "In the midst of lovemaking or conver-sation, there's always Jack or Jill phoning up to talk about who's doing what tonight. That's hard on people. You want to be treated in some special way."

That specialness is available in the middle ground of serial monogamy. Winkler, Hickling, and Cragg, all of whom are mar-ried with children, disagree on whether serial monogamy can be ethical. But they're probably not as far apart as it first seems.

All recognize keeping a series of partners creates compli-cations. Sexually transmitted disease is the most obvious.

With AIDS and 25 other sexually transmitted diseases raging through North America, lives are in danger every time new partners engage in sex. It's despicable, obviously, to hide a contagious sexual disease from a lover. And every time someone sleeps with a new person, the danger grows of catching, or spreading, more disease.

Serial monogamy might be good for people who are testing how much intimacy they can tolerate, Winkler says. But it's prone to superficiality. At its extreme, serial monogamy is reduced to speedy relationships that can make sex an impersonal act. "In serial monogamy," says Winkler, "you can leave as soon as things threaten your image of yourself. Many things can be left unconfronted."

The early romance of serial relationships is exciting, but Winkler and Hickling believe humans eventually feel drawn to long-term commitment.

"I rejected marriage in my youth, but I came around to it," Winkler says. "I used to resist saying this, but I don't any more: There is a deep tension between the attractiveness of single life and the attractiveness of married life. It's one of the truths of existence that we can't live both ways." ✦

Question box

1. What are the advantages to you of being married, of being single?

2. Do you think recreational sex between consenting partners is okay?

3. Are you able to balance sexual excitement with sexual security in your life? Do you think it's possible?

3. *Moderation in all vices*

Q: At a party, you realize you've put someone down during a heated discussion. Others have heard. You think you made a correct point, but the other person has been rendered red-faced. Do you apologize in front of everyone?

✦ ✦ ✦ ✦ ✦

- Pride
- Gluttony
- Greed
- Envy
- Anger
- Sloth
- Lust

Sound like titles for upcoming Madonna videos.

Sorry, couldn't resist. Still, you've got to admit the egotistical mega-star symbolizes a kind of moral abandon infecting the Western psyche these days, making most of us chuckle at mere mention of the bad old Seven Deadly Sins.

Vice is just not something over which people can get a really solid conversation going nowadays. What's happened to naming our dark qualities? To taking a hard look at humans' capacity for wrong? Although virtue is not entirely dead in the late 20th century, it certainly seems to have gone underground. Most seem shy to admit they try to avoid being bad. Is it not hip to be good?

In medieval times, the Seven Deadly Sins were big time, right up there with the Ten Commandments. Passed on to the West by a monk named John Cassian about A.D. 400, the seven went in and out of favor before Chaucer and Dante took them up. In the 1400s, the stern artistic genius Hieronymus Bosch painted ordinary men and women reveling in these primary sins. Gluttony and anger and their ilk became personified in allegory tales and as castle gargoyles.

Maybe now — just maybe — with society's moral compass veering madly all over the map, with the Material Girl representing so much that's out of whack about our values, we are less eager to snicker away these seven vices. They are certainly not irrelevant to modern times. They connect to shopping-mall culture, environmental sustainability, physical and sexual abuse, hurtful competition, addiction, and relationship-destroying cynicism. Not to mention crime in the streets.

And anyway, in a time when everything we do seems to get ranked in Top 10s, it's hard to resist a list, especially one so blunt. Actually, that's part of what made the Seven Deadly Sins valuable, says Catholic scholar Paul Burns. The beauty of the Seven Deadly Sins is their simplicity: seven words. In early times, a list freed up the individual who couldn't read. "A list encouraged people to be masters of their own moral conscience."

Throughout history, the Seven Deadly Sins have been viewed as those that threaten one's relationship with the divine source of life, says Burns, who teaches comparative religion. For those who don't want to look at the seven sins under the harsh light of possible divine retribution, one of North America's leading ethicists emphasizes it's still valuable to look at them as undesirable character traits.

Michael McDonald views things such as pride and greed as natural tendencies that can get out of hand, powerful emotions that can carry us away, create chaos. They are potential vices that need to be controlled, he says, because they interfere with our capacity to make sound moral judgments.

"They're worse when they're the result of long years of neglect and bad habit," McDonald says. Negative traits can become a part of people, who become automatically greedy, or automatically angry — just blowing up at anything. "The people who are unaware of their vices," McDonald says, "can do the most damage."

A marriage and family therapist also says it's valuable to remember the traditional seven vices. Vince D'Monte says many of the troubled people who pick up the phone for a psychologist are captured by difficulties rooted in things such as gluttony and lust. Although D'Monte rarely uses the word sin in counseling because it turns off so many, he's sympathetic to the traditional idea that the Seven Deadly Sins pinpoint personality characteristics that spawn disorder. "Most clients are involved in a struggle of good and evil that's going on right there inside them."

While magazine-rack psychology has encouraged many people to blame their own bad acts on crummy parents, D'Monte thinks it's important to attempt to take responsibility for yourself when you act like a jerk. Keeping in mind the seven vices can help you do that.

But.

And this is the first of many buts. There is another side, a complementary pole, to each one of these seven vices. Avoiding wrong — doing right — is not that simple in this paradoxical, yin-yang world. Catholic scholar Burns, philosopher McDonald, and psychologist D'Monte, all of whom bring warmth and genuine caring to their professions, suggest there can be a good side to lust, pride, envy, etc.

"We have to accept the gestalt," says D'Monte. "We always like to take just one side, but to be fully human, I have to accept that I am capable of both good and bad. When I accept that, I am accepting all of my humanness."

As the ancient Greek philosopher Aristotle said, the point of life is to avoid extremes, to practice moderation. In this case, that attitude leads to recognizing and working with feelings of greed or anger, but avoiding being overwhelmed by them. Since sin can be as complex as human nature, each one of the seven warrants a closer look.

Pride

Pride has traditionally been ranked the gravest vice. "It's failure to recognize that ultimate goodness or greatness comes from something other than yourself," says Burns. Pride spawns the conceit of those who credit themselves solely for their accomplishments, the arrogance of a ruling elite, the smugness of a self-satisfied religious devotee, the selfishness of a family that looks out only for itself.

Therapist D'Monte agrees that pride plays a part in most wrong-doing. People aware of pride's danger are more likely to have a better view of their place in the universe. "When I'm aware of the dangers of pride, I know I can't say I'm superior to you in any way," D'Monte says. Clients hooked by pride, D'Monte says, have a tough time activating one of life's greatest healing responses: forgiveness. Prideful people find it nearly impossible to ask for forgiveness from those they've harmed. It's hard to say you're sorry.

There's another face of pride, however: Some people don't have enough of it. They lack self-esteem. They're not self-assertive. They put themselves down. The trick with pride, and all the sins, is not to totally deny it, but to avoid its excesses.

Gluttony

Now, here's a sin contemporary people can get worked up about. In these health-conscious, environmentally attuned times, overindulgence in food, drink, drugs, and the planet's resources presses a big red NO button. But the fashionability of gluttony as a vice should not lead to puritanism.

"Food is very good. The pleasures of the senses are very good. I would not want to deprive myself totally," D'Monte says. Even the ascetic, Saint Francis of Assisi, upon learning he was about to die in his mid-forties, concluded he had been much too harsh on his body (which he called Brother Ass), D'Monte says. In his final days, Saint Francis allowed Brother Ass to revel in culinary delights.

Greed

Greed has a way of giving rise to injustice. Excessive greed, an unhealthy emphasis on collecting worldly possessions, generates blindness to the needs and rights of others. Greed (also called avarice) creates a disordered, imbalanced life. Problems arise when people want too much, too fast. Greedy people are clueless about fairness and sharing.

However, in measured doses, greed can be okay, says D'Monte. "To be human I must have a natural urge to acquire something — perhaps a little house."

Envy

Envy is quintessentially 20th century. "The materialism of our times is based very much on the notion of envy," says ethicist McDonald. How would TV executives fill the spots between sit-coms without the lure of envy?

"In our society, which is ordered around the market, envy can be very destructive of human relations and cooperative relationships," McDonald says. Perhaps because he works in academia, where discussion has a way of turning viciously competitive, McDonald confesses he's particularly bothered by envy that leads to malicious acts against people of merit.

"I find it personally disturbing when people make themselves feel good by tearing other people down. It's puffed-up self-importance. Rather than making themselves better, they try to make other people less."

Then again, twinges of envy can be beneficial. Envy can lure people to better themselves — to strive for a thing or quality someone else possesses. Says D'Monte: "Good envy tells you: 'He's done so well, maybe I could too.'"

Anger

Given this era in which people, particularly women, are encouraged to express their anger, this is a sin that needs to be carefully interpreted. Appropriate anger tells you how to protect your boundaries — to avoid someone walking all over you. "If you don't allow yourself to feel anger, no healing is possible. You need to confront people with anger, tell them they've hurt you," says D'Monte.

"Anger and rage are totally different things. When anger is kept in, it explodes into rage. That's not helpful. It batters people. No one is left with dignity. Relationships are cut off." When a wrong is being done to you or another, an angry response can be desirable. "But a pattern of self-indulgent rage is very destructive," Burns says. "One has to accept some responsibility for it — by helping to remedy any hurt that's been caused."

Sloth

Laziness. This means more than just sloughing off household chores or job assignments. "It's failure to take responsibility in an area of one's life," says Burns. "It's ethical sloth. It can be extended to mean showing a lack of responsibility for one's family and for ignoring one's obligations to the neighborhood or the community," says Burns.

In an age of workaholism, however, the opposite of sloth also has its dangers. "The other extreme is the person who cannot play," says D'Monte. "You have to work, but there's also a time to slow down and smell the roses."

Lust

Did someone just scream the vice used to market so many people and products? Desire has a positive function to perform in human relationships. But an immature approach to desire leads to people losing themselves to lust. That can harm the rights of many people from cheated spouses to sex-abuse victims to objectified partners.

Like most vices, lust throws lives out of balance. Many people with problems approach lust like impatient children seeking immediate gratification, D'Monte says. "I think some of us have not learned to wait."

✦ ✦ ✦ ✦ ✦

It's worthwhile to ponder the seven vices. But, in the end, it could be more valuable to contemplate the positive: virtue. We tend to associate ethics with feeling bad, says McDonald. But we should start associating ethics with feeling good about ourselves — in a way that looks toward ethical excellence.

Rather than hammering on sins, we should encourage integrity: in families, schools, and workplaces. "We need to conjure up the notion of being a whole person, being aware of our effect on others, and having a sense of inward direction, of holding our values in the face of all these vices," says McDonald.

So.... We began with a list of the bad. Let's challenge Madonna's tawdriness and finish by holding up a list of the

good — the traditional seven virtues of Western philosophy.
For your consideration:

- Moderation
- Discretion
- Courage
- Justice
- Trust
- Hope
- And, perhaps the greatest of these, Love.✦

Question box

1. Which of the seven vices are you most vulnerable to? Do greed, envy, lust, et al. ever interfere with your ability to make a sound choice?

2. Could you gain from being less hard on yourself? Is there room for you to feel a little more pride about what you've done? Or to allow yourself a moment of laziness to smell the roses?

3. Which virtues do you value the most? Why?

4. When does human life begin?

Q: Your teenage daughter comes to you and tells you she's pregnant. Do you help her obtain an abortion?

◆ ◆ ◆ ◆ ◆

It's ironic: In these supposedly materialistic times, one of the most contentious debates of the era centers on a philosophical point — one that's frustratingly elusive.

The topic — when human life begins — goes well beyond the polite give-and-take of dinner-party chatter. It is most painfully coming alive over the abortion issue, with pro-life advocates claiming a human being is created at the moment of conception.

New reproductive technologies, which bring together a woman's egg and a man's sperm in a laboratory to create an embryo, also fuel the debate, which usually resembles fiery warfare rather than a reasoned exchange of views. Catholics and most evangelicals oppose reproductive technology, saying it fails to respect an embryo as a person. Their opponents counter passionately that reproductive technology holds out hope for infertile couples and can screen genetic defects so women don't have to give birth to diseased babies.

Opinion polls show most North Americans want a consistent definition of when life begins so that abortions could be stopped after that stage. But abortion laws differ across the continent. Many courts rule that the fetus is not a legal person until it fully emerges from the birth canal. But to many other people, that's dead wrong.

Society's clash over the origins of humanity — though by no means restricted to churchgoers — has long and perplexing roots. Although the Bible took a life-affirming view of the world, it contains no clear-cut prohibition of elective abortion, according to a useful booklet called *What About Abortion?*, prepared by the Process and Faith Center, which is connected to Claremont Graduate School in California.

This book says that the Bible does include some suggestions that life begins at conception, but contrary to popular belief, contains even stronger indications that it begins at birth. "Biblical tradition," it says, "regards the unborn human life as valuable, but not fully a human until it has emerged from the womb and drawn breath."

For much of its history, the Catholic church was guided by the teaching of 13th-century theologian Saint Thomas Aquinas, who taught that an embryo becomes human only as it develops in the womb. The human soul, Aquinas said, was not infused into the embryo until about the 40th day for males, and about the 80th day for females. The Catholic hierarchy did not overrule Aquinas' teaching until 1869, when the Vatican decreed that a human person is created at conception and called for a ban on all abortions.

For roughly 100 years, this Catholic view influenced the United States and Canada to turn abortion into a criminal offense. Now abortion laws are in a state of flux in North America, and the worldwide Christian church remains divided on the issue, with some denominations saying abortion is sometimes the lesser of two evils — an unfortunate necessity.

Given the lack of agreement among Christians and other religions on the origins of personhood, many probe science for what they hope will be a certain answer. But science cannot prove when a developing cell mass becomes a human, says David Suzuki, a noted geneticist who hosted the recent public-television series, *The Secret of Life*. Science can only provide a biological context for debate. A newly fertilized egg contains a genetic blueprint called DNA, Suzuki says, that has only the "potential" for humanness. "We would not call an architectural blueprint and all of the construction materials a house," he says, "until after its construction."

What About Abortion? also agrees that an embryo consists of potential, "and since one cannot murder a potential person, but only actual persons, the language of murder for abortion is inaccurate." However, after eight weeks gestation, when an embryo becomes a fetus and starts to develop a central nervous system, *What About Abortion?* says the fetus has a strong, albeit ambiguous, claim to personhood.

The religion writer for *The New York Times*, Peter Steinfels, has taken the central nervous system argument further and suggested prohibiting abortion after eight weeks. "At this point all organs are present that will later be developed fully," he says, "and the unborn individual has a distinctly human appearance." Although Steinfels says his argument "is not that [eight weeks] is the 'magic moment' when 'human life begins,'" he believes it is when a majority of North Americans should be compelled to agree that the unborn deserve legal protection.

Reflecting the views of many who hold to a later genesis of the human being, a prominent abortion-rights activist, Hilda Thomas, says "you have to think about personhood" at the time at which a premature infant has a chance of surviving outside the womb — roughly 22 weeks. There's no doubt an embryo is human *life*, Thomas says, but it does not grow into a human *being* until much later. (Ninety percent of abortions in the United States and Canada are conducted before 12 weeks.)

The debate over when a human person originates touches us to our marrow. It seems to speak of our own worth as humans. For now, however, pinpointing the actual magic moment when personhood begins appears speculative. There are, as they say, no easy answers — other than it seems an early abortion is superior to a late one.

But with the controversy currently boiling in a vitriolic rage, with opponents finding each other not only wrong but morally repugnant, consensus is highly unlikely. Perhaps the best for which we can hope is that everyone entering the debate do so with compassion and humility. It's hard to disagree with the advice in *What About Abortion?* to carry out debate about the origins of the person with "an openness to our opponent as one who also struggles with the issue in the depths of his or her being. The answers are not as clear as either side would like to say.... We dare not damn the other, for perhaps in this ambiguous situation it is the other, not ourselves, who has the best judgment."✦

Question box

1. When, roughly, do you think human life begins?

2. Would you allow your 16-year-old daughter to make up her own mind about whether to have an abortion?

3. How do you think people should decide whether to have an abortion? How could someone be a positive influence on helping a woman decide whether to have an abortion?

5. Dying with dignity

Q: Your close relative has always said he doesn't want to die in hospital. He asks you to collect the pills that, if taken all at once, will end his life and cut short his terminal illness. Do you?

✦ ✦ ✦ ✦ ✦

Alzheimer's disease is eating away your elderly mother's brain cells. In lucid moments, she correctly realizes she faces irreversible dementia. The disease will pound her with uncontrollable anxiety, bouts of rage, and disorientation. She'll lose control of her bodily functions, she'll go blind and probably lash out violently. She knows she'll be a heavy burden.

She wants to die.

This agonizing dilemma is being faced among families every day now as modern science has discovered countless ways to keep loved one's hearts, stomachs, and lungs indefinitely pumping — while degenerative diseases keep them constantly suffering.

Outside religious circles, the right to die hasn't posed a huge philosophical problem. It has long been secular humanists' contention that terminally ill people should have the right to die. "The humanistic tradition asks: what separates a human being from animals? The standard answer, since Aristotle, has been: Our capacity for rationality and free will," says Earle Winkler, co-author of *Applied Ethics: A Reader.* "So, if somebody faces an awful future of pain, decline, and the deterioration of the very capacities that make them human, and they decide to direct their own fate, then the humanistic tradition views this as a kind of courageous expression of these capacities."

The main source of opposition to the right to die lies in the traditional religious beliefs that human life is absolutely sacred, and we don't own our lives — God does. Many religious groups have eloquently stood up for positions similar to that of the influential 13th-century theologian Thomas Aquinas. While agreeing that God gives humans free will in most aspects of life, Aquinas said, "The passage from this life to a more blessed one is not a matter subject to man's free will, but to God's power. A man may not, therefore, kill himself in order to escape from any of the miseries of this life."

With medical technology keeping bodies functioning longer and longer in the 20th century, public opinion polls show Aquinas' stand has been losing ground. In the early 1980s, only 40% of North Americans backed the right to die (which is technically different from euthanasia, which involves someone else doing the killing). Now, more than 70% support the right to die.

The mounting rejection of the theologian's stand has come at the same time people are questioning the authority of religious leaders. Then again, polls also show more than four out of five North Americans still believe in God, and almost as many consider themselves Christian. Whether we recognize it or not, most of those who have changed their mind on the right to die must be looking at it against some spiritual backdrop.

In this hotly contested debate, contemporary thinkers have come up with numerous responses to those who would say you don't have the right to allow your ailing mother to put a final end to her suffering. Some adopt the position taken by David Hume, the famous 18th-century Scottish empiricist, in his essay, "On Suicide." Hume reasoned that if God is merciful and gave humans rationality and free will, then God would allow humans to use those cherished faculties in dire circumstances.

Even though traditional theologians have said humans have no right to "play God" with life and death, other philosophers say we do it all the time. Humans have played God by launching revolution for social change, by prolonging life through medicine, by avoiding unwanted babies, by killing people in war.

"Theologically, few now would accept the view that one range of actions belongs wholly to the sphere of human free will and another wholly to God," writes noted American philosopher-theologian John Cobb, in his book, *Matters of Life and Death*. "God is at work everywhere, in a way that does not set aside the decisions of the creatures. Instead, God makes such decisions possible and works in and through them."

Most people stand up for the idea that human life is sacred, or to put it in non-religious terms, deserving of respect. You only have to look at Nazi Germany to view the horrors that occur when some humans are excluded from such a commitment. But again, while some say the inviolability of human life means no one can kill themselves, few people consistently uphold the absolute sacredness of human life. They would be willing to kill someone, for example, who tried to murder their child.

Rather than trying to be absolutistic about the sacredness of human life, Cobb says it's better for spiritual people to build on the New Testament teaching that God loves all people, and people should love one another. "Love can usually be best expressed by allowing that other human being to realize her or his own projects, so far as these do not prevent other persons from realizing their projects also."

That doesn't mean people have the right to do whatever they want with their lives. It doesn't allow a depressed, middle-aged man with a family to support to do himself in, for example. Even if the man's life is filled with pain, he has the obligation to struggle through his problems rather than escape them and impose greater hardships on his family. On the other hand, chances are high that a woman succumbing to Alzheimer's disease could be acting responsibly to others and herself by choosing to end her life with dignity and without pain.

Another classic argument against the right to die is that taking one's own life is unnatural. But while the theory of "natural law" can be useful, it can also be repressive. It can lead to questionable conclusions, such as sex is only natural when it's done in the interest of procreation, whereas sex for mutual enjoyment is unnatural. Although it does seem natural for people to cling to life, Cobb suggests it is perhaps just as natural that people who have enjoyed living for 70, 80, or 90 years do not cling so desperately to it. "Perhaps it is according to nature that at some point people are ready to die, and perhaps it is 'against nature' to protract life beyond that point when health, or mind, has failed."

Another important objection to the right to die is the so-called slippery-slope argument. It says we must absolutely forbid an ailing person's right to die because it may encourage us to devalue human life. It may even lead us to badger an ill person into committing suicide for the sake of our own convenience. Those who support the right to die respond by saying strong moral and legal codes must be established that affirm the right of the terminally ill to take their own life, without undercutting a belief in the preciousness of every person.

Legal safeguards against erratic death decisions could include having doctors verify that patients who choose to die are acting with clear minds and of their own free will, requiring waiting periods for those who say they want to die, and perhaps calling for the agreement of a majority of loved ones. Having more people involved in your sick mother's decision to die is designed to reduce, not increase, the likelihood of ending life.

The right-to-die debate becomes even more contentious when it's put in a wider context that looks at things such as the high cost to society of maintaining the life of someone who wants to die. A planet groaning under unsustainable consumption levels should not reject ethical ways to reduce the pressure, says Cobb. "Allowing more freedom of choice about life and death would be one way, less horrible than some alternatives, to do this."

In the midst of your sadness, how do you do the right thing for your pain-wracked mother who wants to die? These philosophers say it requires coming to the realization that respecting her life means respecting her choices.◆

Question box

1. Have you known any terminally ill people who have wanted to take their own lives? How do you feel about what they did?

2. Do you think human beings have the right to "play God" by supporting someone who wants to end their life? Why?

3. What is the best way to show love to an ailing person who wants to die?

6. A meaty issue

Q: You eat chicken at home. While visiting a friend's farm, you're asked if you want to help kill some chickens for dinner. Do you?

✦ ✦ ✦ ✦ ✦

Grammy Award winning singer k.d. lang lassoed a feisty topic when she appeared in a TV ad against eating meat. The ethics surrounding food animals weigh heavily on the scales. Almost 90% of North Americans still dine on meat, poultry, and fish. The rights of food animals — which are easy to block out when scanning a menu — involve billions of creatures, people, and dollars.

We are nowhere near fulfilling Leonardo da Vinci's prophecy that "the time will come when men such as I look on the murder of animals as they now look on the murder of men." But with a Gallup poll showing a majority of North Americans feel sympathy for the animal-rights movement, with red-meat consumption slipping, and with Sweden bringing in legislation to protect farm animals, it's plain the issue has the power of an electric prod.

If you doubt it, take note: A billboard outside lang's home town of Consort, Alberta, was defaced after word came out about her "Meat Stinks" ad. Some radio stations banned her music; meat producers denounced vegetarianism as a fad, and lang's stand has been fussed over countless times on popular TV shows such as *Entertainment Tonight*.

The rights of food animals have given ethics professor Earle Winkler increasingly more trouble since he's been forced to think hard about them for his course on environmental ethics. He's cut his meat consumption, but still hasn't given it up completely.

"There are so many really significant human issues associated with the raising of animals for food," Winkler says. "There would be a major upheaval in human terms if we were to turn en masse to vegetarianism. A lot of people would be out of work. But it's not only the money, there's the tradition associated with cattle raising and sheep raising. It's so close to home because all but vegetarians are involved in the exploitation of these critters."

The food-animal rights debate boils down to three key questions:

- Can we justify killing animals?
- If we choose to put flesh on the barbecue, is there a difference between serving up a pig or a fish?
- How should we treat animals we've destined for slaughter?

Many true vegetarians believe all sentient beings (creatures capable of feeling and thinking) have an unquestionable right to life. This morality, although inherent in some Eastern religions, moves into rough terrain, practically, when it comes to things such as whether to swat mosquitoes.

Some philosophers maintain humans dwell on a higher plane than animals, who don't have an absolute right to life. Winkler makes a distinction between humans, who have self-consciousness, and animals, who many argue have "mere consciousness." (This is not a completely secure ethical position, Winkler admits. American ethicists such as Tom Regan argue that many animals have more self-consciousness than some severely retarded humans, whose right to life we vehemently support. "Regan," Winkler says, "would say making a distinction between human and animal consciousness is pure self-serving prejudice.")

Even long-time animal-rights activists don't necessarily push stringent vegetarianism. The head of Citizens for the Ethical Treatment of Animals, for example, eats fish. "Everybody has to find their own level" regarding how much animal flesh to eat, says Tina Harrison, a former board member of the Society for the Prevention of Cruelty to Animals. Although Harrison believes vegetarians who avoid all animal products, such as milk and eggs, are more evolved than meat eaters, she'll eat salmon and cod because she believes fish don't feel to the same extent as four-footed animals. "They don't have the same susceptibility to pain as land animals because their central nervous system and physiological structure is not as sophisticated," Harrison said. When a hooked fish flaps and gasps on the line, she believes it's displaying a reflex reaction.

On the other hand, the author of the best-selling vegetarian manifesto, *Diet for a New America,* says studies have shown pigs are as intelligent as dogs. John Robbins would like to see us include pigs (and cows and lambs) in the punchy aphorism lang used in her TV ad: "We all love animals, but why do we call some pets and some dinner?"

Ethically, Harrison and Winkler also urge us to create a continuum that makes distinctions between species' sophistication. They believe animals with greater psychological complexity, such as pigs, have a strong claim to human's moral consideration.

Although animal-rights advocates disagree on certain aspects of their cause, one thing is clear to all of them: cows, pigs, chickens, turkeys, and other creatures that end up on our table are capable of suffering — and they shouldn't suffer any more than necessary. "They're capable of feeling tremendous fear, when their mothers are taken away or they're kept forever in the dark," Harrison says. "What we do to animals reflects on ourselves. I think it's demeaning to humans that animals be treated as if they were unfeeling factory machinery."

Although meat industry representatives question the charges, Harrison, Winkler, and numerous others say the food-animal industry crams farm animals into small cages their entire lives, force feeds them antibiotics, and deliberately makes veal cows anemic so their meat will be tender.

In light of such treatment, Winkler and Harrison find appeal in a philosophical attitude that affirms the sanctity of all life. Native Indians, they say, believe it possible to take animal life, as long as humans show an attitude of reverence and respect for the sacrificed beasts.

Harrison keeps in mind the saying by Albert Schweitzer, who received the Nobel Prize for Peace: "Any religion which is not based on respect for life is not a true religion ... Until humans extend their circle of compassion to all living things, they will not themselves find peace."✦

Question box

1. Which animals do you like the most?

2. Which do you think have more value? Dogs, pigs, fish, insects?

3. If you eat meat, do you think that's okay? Why?

4. How could we show reverence for animals destined for slaughter?

---

7. *Women, men, and power*

Q: You and a friend have applied to win a scholarship. During your interview, one of the judges, who is of the opposite sex, unfairly criticizes your friend. Do you defend your friend?

✦ ✦ ✦ ✦ ✦

Oops. Men appear to be blowing it in the ethics department. Far be it from me to promote the popular pastime of criticizing men (some of my best friends are men), but two new studies reveal a hard-to-ignore tendency among those of the male persuasion.

A recent in-depth public opinion survey exploring the social mores of more than 2,000 people came to the firm conclusion that women generally act more ethically than men. "Women are the more moral sex. That's one of the only propositions that the two sexes absolutely agree upon," say James Patterson and Peter Kim, the public-opinion researchers who wrote the new book, *The Day America Told the Truth.*

"Women are morally superior to men. This is true everywhere, in every single region, on every moral issue we tested," say the blunt authors (both males, take note). "Women lie less. Women are more responsible. Women can be trusted more. It is imperative that women be looked to for leadership in America right now in government, in politics, in religion, in education, in business."

Before any readers have a conniption, they should keep in mind that *The Day America Told the Truth* amounts to a study of statistical averages. It does not say individual men cannot be more ethical than women. And it does not state all women are saints. The sweeping survey by Patterson and Kim has special weight, however, because every man and woman who spent a day answering its more than 1,000 questions could be brutally honest; they were protected by anonymity.

Here's a taste of the findings on ethics among the sexes:

- Twenty-five percent of men have stolen from a stranger, compared to six percent of women.

- Sixty-three percent of men have lied to protect themselves, compared to 52% of women.

- Fifteen percent of men have been drunk at work, compared to four percent of women.

- Forty-three percent of men have cheated on an exam, compared to 27% of women.

- Fifty percent of men believe "politics," rather than hard work, is the way to get ahead, compared to 42% of women.

- Fifty-six percent of men have challenged someone to a fight, compared to 26% of women.

- Young men commit the vast majority of violent crimes.

This is not merely a U.S. phenomenon. One of Canada's top analysts of shifting ethical sands, sociologist Reginald Bibby, confirms women frequently outdistance men when it comes to upholding values and principles.

"There's no question you get a picture of women in Canada that show them, frankly, as being a lot nicer than us guys," said Bibby. "Women come across much more compassionate, much more sensitive, much more concerned about anything that has a human variable in it."

One reason the authors of *The Day America Told the Truth* urge more women to move into the traditionally male worlds of business and politics is to counteract one of the survey's other major findings: We believe society is going down the tubes because people are confused and disagreeing about right and wrong.

The number-one reason North America is in economic decline, say those surveyed, is low ethics among business executives. "Greed in American management is out of control. Never have so many taken so much, right off the top," says the book. Managers' view of their own morality is even lower than employees' opinion of managers' morality. Employees' attitudes also leave much room for improvement.

"But though our current ethics at work are low, they'd be a lot worse if not for the greater number of women who have entered the workforce in recent years," says the book. "Women are much less willing to compromise their values to get ahead and somewhat more willing to quit as a matter of principle if they learn that their company is engaging in illegal activities."

Despite the authors' discovery that women are "overwhelmingly" more ethical than men in their personal and work lives, females have a few weak points. Sometimes the statistical differences between the ethical leanings of men and women are not huge.

Women are also more suspicious than men, leading to questionable acts. Fifty-six percent of women have secretly searched through a man's wallet, for example, compared to only 34% of men who have done the same through a woman's purse. And longstanding "bad attitudes" between the sexes remain intact. Women and men still grotesquely stereotype one another; many women see men as uniformly dumb or admit to using men strictly for money or sex. And men tend to feel that while they're trying hard to understand women these days, women are not reciprocating.

The Day America Told the Truth, however, falls short on exploring why women generally act more ethically than men. However, Margaret Fulton, retired president of Mount Saint Vincent University in Halifax, thought the survey results reflected how men, more than women, have been socialized to be competitive and strive for power.

"Men have to be strong. Men have to fight. They have to be tough. They have to go into the sports arena. They have to throw people on the boards," Fulton said. A desire for power over others, she said, usually leads to lower ethics. At the top of society's hierarchy, there's also tremendous pressure on both men and women to conform to the standard ethically shaky methods of attaining and maintaining personal power.

While women without power become manipulative, Fulton says women who play the power game often become as immoral as the worst man. Former British prime minister Margaret Thatcher and Israeli leader Golda Meir weren't significantly different from male leaders. "The trouble for women is if you don't participate like other members of the power group you're in, you're asking for crucifixion."

Guy Corneau, author of *Absent Fathers, Lost Sons: The Search for Masculine Identity,* says the two sets of survey results do not necessarily prove men are fundamentally immoral, but instead point to men's psychological wounds. He says the surveys show men who are unsure about their male identity and have not learned to express feelings frequently try to prove they're macho by acting out. They drink, fight, do drugs, beat up partners, cheat, and steal.

"When men feel bad, they don't know what to do. Their fathers often haven't even been around enough to teach them how to express emotions in a healthy way or to be spontaneous or sensitive," says Corneau. "Although I don't find the survey results surprising, I would hope they wouldn't be used to bash men. I hope they would encourage people to understand men from the inside."✦

1. Do you think psychological wounds can cause men, and women, to act less ethically? Has that been true for you?

2. Does pressure to be tough, or succeed at work, require you to compromise your scruples? What could you do about it?

3. What could you do to center your life, so you could face ethical challenges with more integrity and self-control?

4. Do you think there's a need for gender reconciliation? What could men and women learn from each other?

Part 2
Community ties

The community stagnates without the impulse of the individual. The impulse dies without the sympathy of the community.

William James

✦ ✦ ✦ ✦ ✦

Tired of fast food, fast lanes, and fast lives, we're pressing on the brakes and slowing down. Rather than rushing to be somewhere else, we're checking out where we are. We're realizing we can't just look out for ourselves (and perhaps our nuclear families). We're connected to something larger: our communities. We're getting to know our neighbors and joining citizens' groups like never before: talking about schools, traffic, the media, medical care, politicians, air pollution, panhandlers, local business, and kids' sports. We're finding out you care for yourself when you care for those around you.

8. Putting down roots

Q: After signing up your young child for a sport, you're asked to help coach her team. You used to play the sport yourself. Do you agree to help out?

✦ ✦ ✦ ✦ ✦

I have often relied on the kindness of strangers — or at least those who owed me nothing. As a kid, I was raised by a whole bunch of people. I was raised by the neighborhood.

My mother took a full-time job after a tragedy left her a single parent. While she bore main parenting duties, the people who inhabited the block where we lived did much to shape my soul. My uncle lived with us, becoming a male role model. My brother watched out for me. My grandmother was there for emergencies.

Neighborhood moms took me in at any and all times. Friends taught me how to play baseball, go trick-or-treating, and have rock fights using garbage can lids as shields. We kids dominated the block like a mob of fondly regarded rabbits. While this informal style of child-rearing probably had something to do with my leg, wrist, and nose being broken by age five on various unsupervised outings with buddies, it also had a lot to do with me, decades later, treasuring my roots, treasuring community.

Many fortunate people can tell similar stories about communities that gave them a sense of who they are in the world, about groups that gelled in a wondrous way, about a bunch of disparate individuals who somehow formed an intimate, seemingly unbreakable bond. These experiences of community reflect what many philosophers consider the essence of life: to be interconnected, to be in relationship, to be known, to belong, to have a sense of home.

Various communities have given my life meaning — from old high school friends to a small group-oriented liberal arts program at university called Arts One, from an Ontario theater company to a lively campus ministry network. I've found communities, or they've found me, despite social forces conspiring against it.

If the chemistry is right, community can happen anywhere: a city block, a small town, a church or temple, a classroom, a retreat center, a club, a self-help group, a coffee klatsch, a team, a restaurant hang-out, or even a workplace. Because it's so basic, often we don't even know we've had community until it's gone.

A global economy produces unstable jobs, demands mobile workers. TV encourages private lives. Commuting keeps us unattached. Suburban sprawl lacks gathering places. Rampant consumerism keeps us trying to buy a lifestyle, rather than live one. Competing turns colleagues into enemies. And rugged individualism gets us thinking no one will take care of us; we have to do it ourselves, perhaps ruthlessly.

But something's happening. Baby boomers are settling down after flitting around the world to schools, jobs, experiences, and fancy hotels. They're committing themselves to families and neighborhoods, putting down roots and getting involved. Some analysts say North Americans are joining community groups like never before. People are tiring of yearning for one place while living in another.

"Where do I belong? Where are my roots?" asks Brad Edmondson, editor of *American Demographics* magazine. "Today this question is becoming acute for me and many of the people I know. As a I muddle from youth into middle age, the realization is dawning that this is not merely a rehearsal. This is the one life I have on earth. So I wonder: Where is the best place to spend the time I have? Where is my true home?"

I've had exciting times living in Toronto and Los Angeles —adventurous, demanding, and even dangerous times. There are far more vibrant, powerful, important places than Vancouver, where I live now. But unless economic necessity dictates otherwise, I'm here for the long run. With my wife and three sons, we'll stay on the same block in the same small, disheveled (now over-priced) house. Our next-door neighbors, Mrs. Fisher and daughter Jane, and Mary on the other side, have been there a long, long time and tolerate our kids turning their front yards into a baseball field. We'll hold more neighborhood parties, where attendees range from 18 months of age to somewhere in the eighties. We've twice obtained city approval to barricade the street against cars so we can hold summer block parties.

It's the little things that make community. By staying put, our children can get to know their grandparents, aunts and uncles, cousins, great-aunts and great-uncles. We also get some free babysitting and Sunday dinners, which go a long way to offering some semblance of well-being. Like thousands of other fathers and mothers, I coach kids' soccer and baseball teams. With neighbors, I've become a bicycle activist, lobbying city hall to make the city more human by building a network of bicycle routes on side streets. We've had some successes. Along with more than 500 others, we also won a battle to save four of the city's aptly named community schools.

As for old-time roots, I get together each month for dinner and conversation with men friends from university days. The family's summer vacation amounts to something of a *Big Chill* experience (without the funeral). We meet for a few weeks at a generous friend's cabin with people who come from all across North America to talk, cook, swim, talk, fish, do chores, and talk.

Don't get the impression this is idyllic. That's not the nature of community or humans. We endure our share of discord, squabbling, drudgery, pettiness, and misunderstanding — more than you'd get tuning into your TV and CD player, or hunting for just the right pair of shoes at the mall. But last I heard, this is natural: life comes with a certain amount of stress. As church people say, it's easy to love God and one's neighbor in the abstract. The challenge comes in joining a community and loving imperfect people, maintaining ethics in a messy world.

The lifestyle I have is nowhere near as intense as community can be. It's just our nuclear family in our house. We aren't members of a commune or tight-knit religious body. We don't house the poor. We don't even co-own our lawn mower with a neighbor. But we sort of feel connected. It's our tiny challenge to the dominant culture, which seems to want to compartmentalize us, cut us off from our roots, homelands, families, and communities — because that would make us better consumers and more pliable citizens.

If we truly began thinking globally, acting locally, profound ramifications could befall the planet. Stronger commitments to roots would lead to fewer community-destroying policies from powerful people who live beyond the effects. We would see less tolerance for pollution as citizens take responsibility for their bio-region; less psychological alienation; less drug and alcohol abuse; reduced crime; more loyal employees and greater support for local businesses.

That's the big picture. But, for me, community comes most alive in the details: At a good party (with dancing, if the mood is right), with a Saturday morning chat over the back fence with Mrs. Fisher, and with just being there when one of the neighborhood kids learns, for the first time, how to hit a baseball.✦

9. *Healthy competition*

Q: You hear that fellow students are going to cheat on a crucial exam. A foolproof method of cheating is offered to you. Do you cheat because everyone else is?

✦✦✦✦✦

The other coach was too far into it. He had been telling his soccer players how to fool our team with trick plays. With a big grin, he had joked about how he'd beaten us last time (forgetting it was a tie). And when his team popped a ball into our net, he sprinted the length of the field with his index finger in the air — more excited than his six- and seven-year-old players.

Those of us on the opposite side of the mini-soccer field took note, viscerally. Our own competitive urges, which we'd managed to transcend while playing other teams, pumped through our blood like a dozen cups of dark French espresso. To make things worse, the other team was the pushiest we'd ever come across; our kids didn't want to play them. And the volunteer ref, who ignored our requests to do something about the combative play, turned out to be the father of the other team's most belligerent player.

The unrestrained competitiveness tempted us to push our kids harder, yell at them to play more aggressively, and criticize them when they made mistakes; things we'd so far resisted because we wanted to avoid the risk of crushing our kids' spirits.

Whether it's soccer, baseball, hockey, tennis, art, or piano contests, children's competitions bring to a head one of life's most elemental ethical challenges: How will we handle competing?

Many parents think their kids will fail if they don't learn to compete. Some adults argue competition is the bedrock of North American society: getting a job, winning customers, outselling other businesses, prevailing in a court case, bidding for a home, selling a screenplay, obtaining political office, scoring school grades, even striving for the object of one's affection.

Although contests perform useful functions in society, Susan Butt, author of *The Psychology of Sport*, says big problems exist with the "competitive personality." The person who believes winning is everything is intensely egocentric, she says, pointing to a major study. Competitive people are rigid, psychologically defensive, less insightful about themselves, and unable to see others' point of view. In short, Butt says a person who can't control his or her competitive personality is, in many ways, stupid.

The obsessive competitor, Butt says, also often fails to see that cooperation is sometimes the best way for everyone to go. A landmark study, she says, showed competitive personalities, when asked to play a game in which everyone would benefit if they cooperated, would not trust those trying to cooperate. Their mistrust, in turn, forced all players to compete just to survive the game. As a result, all players suffered.

That study contains a big lesson. One boy on our soccer team reacted to the competitive pushiness by kicking one of their kids. Olympic sprinter Ben Johnson, who once held the world record for the 100-meter dash before it was taken away from him, took steroids because he thought other athletes did. People cheat on exams because they hear others are. Politicians misrepresent the truth because they think the opposition lies more. "Competitiveness breeds on itself," says Butt.

"When people start thinking, 'Win at any cost,' then problems arise. If you want to see the human race descend to its lowest level, just get people being competitive."

I have never figured out whether competitiveness is innate or learned. Steeped as a kid in sports, Monopoly, and Cowboys and Indians, I am now quite capable of being competitive. Another reporter ventured one can't be a journalist, prizing scoops and front-page play, without it. Competitiveness seems most pronounced in the oldest of my three sons, who thrives on sports and hangs out with peers who compare what they can do. Yet, my middle son has revealed an all-seeing eye when it comes to how full his glass of juice is compared to his siblings'. And I'm sure when my youngest son was one year old, he would have competed for breast milk; luckily, he was the only one in the race.

The human urge to compete seems to be linked to how animals strive for status in groups, Butt says. The psychologist calls the competitive urge part of our "darker selves," which we need to understand and with which we need to come to terms.

Competition isn't all-pervasive. Some individuals, cultures, and sectors of society are far less competitive than others. And Butt says cooperative individuals and societies, such as the Blackfoot Indians and Inuit, do exist. Most people, at times, are capable of cooperating. On the other hand, competition isn't evil. Without it, there would be no games, says noted ethicist Michael McDonald.

No baseball, races, bridge, bingo, spelling bees, and debating societies. Our communities would be kind of boring without competition. Games, at the very least, can be fun. Contests can also foster individual competence, say Butt and McDonald. Competition can be a motivator. "It encourages us," says McDonald, "to do our best, compete against ourselves." Children are lured forward by matching skills against others of roughly equal or better skills. It's part of the reason,

Butt says, kids who are good at something should not always be held back by being kept with kids with lower skills.

Kids who excel, by competing in teams, can learn to be leaders, says Butt. The best, as long as they don't lord it over others, can be an inspiration to all. Team-oriented competitions, in everything from a hockey game to a company's advertising campaign, can promote collaborating and cooperating, McDonald says. "We learn how to accomplish goals together that we can't accomplish by ourselves."

Keeping such competitions ethical requires vigilance. It's important to avoid skapegoating, particularly when children are involved, says McDonald. Bloodthirsty parents can be awfully hard on kids, often their own, who don't pull their weight on a team. "You hate to see a kid go into a trauma because he missed a goal."

Some competition is immoral simply because of the purpose of the event. In Russian Roulette, the object of the game, a bullet through the brain of the unlucky, is clearly unacceptable, says McDonald. Competition should not become like war, where the goal is to humiliate, injure, or destroy opponents by any means. North American society, for example, has generally decided to show compassion for the fate of the losers in our competitive economic system.

Players must also abide by a contest's rules and take note of the boundaries of play, McDonald says. "The competition has to be restricted to the playing field. You don't hit a player when he's down, you don't take advantage of trust relationships, and you don't disable. There are certain ways individuals shouldn't be treated. When competition causes you to sacrifice the welfare and dignity of individuals, it's gone too far."

The hockey player shouldn't use an oversized stick to get goals, the businessperson shouldn't betray a friend to win a contract, the journalist shouldn't break the law for a front-page story, the lawyer shouldn't mislead a client for a bigger fee and, dare I say, the soccer coach shouldn't allow shin-kicking in hope of sprinting up the field with his finger in the air.✦

Question box

1. What do you think you do more in life: compete or cooperate?

2. Do you think it's realistic to expect more cooperation in society?

3. Is there a chance you might dislike competition because you fear losing?

4. What would you say to a team of children about handling winning and losing, about healthy competition?

10. Charity also begins on the street

Q: A panhandler asks you for a dollar. You think he'll take your money and buy liquor. What do you do?

✦✦✦✦✦

You're downtown for dinner, dressed up a little better than usual. It's not too cold, so you decide to walk, window shop, and cleanse your mind of everyday worries.

Before you cover two blocks, a figure with tattered clothes and a two-day-old beard steps out from a doorway and asks politely as you walk by: "Excuse me. Do you have any spare change?"

Kerblaaaam! You're thrown into an ethical dilemma. And you don't like it. Most people would keep on walking — some without turning a head, without a sound, as if the question was never asked, the person never existed. Others don't miss a step and respond, semi-politely: "No. Sorry." A few stop and place a mish-mash of change in the outstretched hand.

Most of us wonder whether we've done the right thing. The ethical dilemma posed by an approaching panhandler is complex and messy, penetrating to the heart of our personalities and our convictions about how to treat the so-called losers in our community.

Some just don't give a damn about others, says Paul Russell, who has taught ethics at Stanford University and the

University of British Columbia. He says most people — whether politically conservative, centrist, or progressive — share the fundamental principle we all have an obligation to those in need.

The Judeo-Christian roots undergirding the Western world have something to do with that sense of obligation. The highest ideal in Christian thought is charity: to embody divine, unselfish love by showing compassion even to those who might not merit it. Whether or not you hand out a few quarters to a panhandler even if he or she is dirty and turns you off, you've probably been touched by the notion of charity. A lot of us feel twinges of guilt and responsibility when confronted with a panhandler.

Russell usually comes up with the spare change. Although he finds the split-second decision awkward, he believes if you genuinely think the person is in some distress, you should be inclined to help out. He allows himself the privilege of making an instant judgment about the panhandler and whether or not he or she will benefit from a donation. He doesn't usually give to drunks, fearing they'll use it for more booze.

We're often simply annoyed by panhandlers, believing they're lazy or lack discipline or have chosen their lifestyle. But Russell believes society will always have people who need the support of others. Many panhandlers, and many people on welfare, he believes, are mentally or physically disabled or otherwise incapable of holding down regular employment. "It's absurd and heartless to say all these people should get jobs."

It's valid to question whether giving to panhandlers will take away their incentive to get off the street. However, unless passersby begin regularly forking over $20 bills, Russell believes cold temperatures, rain, and the embarrassment of begging are incentive enough to encourage a panhandler to find a better life and eventually contribute to society. Some who don't act charitably to panhandlers disguise their own callousness, Russell says, by convincing themselves not to give for the panhandlers' alleged own good.

The key for Barry Morris, a minister who each day passes numerous outstretched hands in the hard-core urban neighborhoods in which he works, is to offer dignity by acknowledging each panhandler. "They've come out of their 12-by-10 hotel room and their empty hand or hat represents a vital source of contact with the public. It's their way of saying: 'Here I am. Talk to me.'"

When Morris passes a panhandler, he thinks of the John Prine song, "Hello In There." It's about the beauty offered by even minimal human contact. If Morris does not give a panhandler change, a bus ticket, directions to a shelter, or go with him or her for coffee, he at least wishes the person a good day.

Why bother? Beyond showing compassion to an individual, supporting the poorest of the poor helps stop our society from sliding to the anarchic depths of places such as Mexico City or Calcutta, or even New York City. We are all interconnected. It would not take much for increasing homelessness, blight, and poverty-induced crime to seriously reduce the quality of everyone's lives, including the well-off.

The negative side of giving to panhandlers is that it might do little more than give the donor a feel-good buzz. Tossing away an occasional bill can lull people into thinking they've done their bit for society, say Russell and Morris. That could lead to people rationalizing that they don't have to do much else; whether that's working for a charity, lobbying for improvements to the welfare system, or voting for politicians who may redistribute wealth.

A basic reason Morris and Russell usually come with spare change is they've concluded most welfare systems are inadequate. "Short of absolutely superb financial discipline," says Morris, "many on welfare can't help but splurge when their monthly check arrives."

Most of us give to a panhandler hoping it will go to basics such as food or shelter. But Morris' idea of charity extends further. He'll donate so a beggar can enjoy a rare luxury: a movie, a night on the town, or a trip to another city to see a friend.✦

Question box

1. Think of the last time you passed a panhandler. What did you feel?

2. What are the benefits and drawbacks to helping out the poor in our communities?

11. *Getting around means more than getting a license*

Q: You move to a new home near a convenient transit route. Transit will get you to work in 25 minutes. You don't need your car once you're at work. Do you start taking transit?

◆◆◆◆◆

Peter Danielson thinks he's penalized for the way he travels to work. His university subsidizes faculty members who drive cars by providing them with dirt-cheap parking. But professors like himself, who take the bus, do not receive any compensation.

The unintended consequence of university policy, says the ethics specialist, is to encourage car driving. And that, in turn, causes unpleasant traffic jams, noisy neighborhoods, petroleum-related pollution, global warming and, not to put too fine a point on it, the possible destruction of our planet.

The ethics of getting to work have trouble gaining the public's attention in the midst of news about sex crimes, sports stars, shifty politicians, and global mayhem. But for Danielson, his university's relatively minor mistake of subsidizing drivers opens up a trunk load of crucial issues.

In introductory ethics classes, Danielson jumps on traffic congestion to drive home his theories, which lean on the thought of 17th-century British philosopher Thomas Hobbes. "Ethics is the science of what's good for the widest set of interests and how to attain it," says Danielson, who has taught at York University in Toronto. "Ethics is about getting people to think about changing structures."

Following the utilitarian school of philosophy espoused by Hobbes, Danielson says it is not ethics' role to urge people to become moral heroes, who sacrifice themselves (like Jesus or Mahatma Gandhi) to show the world there is a better way to live. The role of ethics, Danielson argues, is to help society create ground rules in which an individual's self-interest will be furthered by pursuing actions that will also benefit the wider community.

Many people currently consider it in their self-interest to drive a car, Danielson says. It's relatively fast and convenient. But ethics, he contends, must encourage laws that make it in a person's self-interest to leave behind the automobile for buses, rapid transit, a bicycle, or walking. Grid-locked traffic and drivers trapped in the isolation of private vehicles now compete in a state of what Hobbes would have called "the brutal state of nature — of all against all," says Danielson. The benefits of reducing car-dependency will include more civilized communities and a less polluted environment.

One simple way to teach the public that cars are not in their self-interest is to reveal how expensive they are. As well as the oppressive cost of buying, maintaining, and insuring a private car, there is the $2,500 to $3,500 per auto that North American taxpayers spend annually for things such as maintaining roads and hiring traffic police. Although enthusiastic about the market economy, Danielson says it has never been able to function without government. There would be no car industry if governments didn't build roads, for example. And the market by itself cannot get people out of cars. Democratic governments, he says, must intensify the incentives, and the often less-expensive penalties and constraints that will push individual car drivers to do the right thing for the sake of themselves and the community.

Since Danielson is a social philosopher, not an urban planner, he leaves much of the details of transportation regulations to others. But one of his modest proposals includes having his university discourage car driving by raising parking fees for faculty members and/or subsidizing bus riders. Other ideas he believes have proved effective elsewhere include slapping higher transportation taxes on gasoline, penalizing single-driver cars by clearing a commuter express lane for vehicles with passengers, and continuing to change zoning so that higher density, and thus cheaper, housing could be built near major work centers.

A person who has dedicated a career to the details of a sweeping vision of a more ecological approach to transportation is Michael Replogle, president of the non-profit Institute for Transportation and Development Policy in Washington. Replogle sees transportation ethics on a grand scale — including how it affects third-world countries.

"Global warming, caused in part by growing motorization, is indisputably occurring and will be one of the biggest problems faced by mankind entering the 21st century. CO_2 emissions, a major source of global warming, continue to grow at more than 4% a year, mostly due to increased automobile use." Replogle writes. "Much of Africa and Latin America continue to be destabilized by huge debts acquired from imports of petroleum and cars used mostly by a small elite. The billions of dollars spent each year to promote motorization for the few leaves less street space and fewer resources for the many who must walk, cycle, or use public transportation."

Replogle travels the world in search of ways to help reduce car dependence. In North America, transportation policies continue to exacerbate petroleum dependency, rather than create environmentally sustainable communities. In Sweden, Germany, the Netherlands, and Japan, numerous creative things have been done to make cities serve humans rather than automobiles. In recent decades, Copenhagen, for example, has retro-fit its streets with a network of segregated bicycle routes, which have drawn 30% of the city's daily commuters on to bicycles. That does not include the many more who pedal to bicycle-friendly mass transit stations.

However, in most North American cities, only about 3% commute by bicycle. Taking a Hobbesian approach to transportation ethics, Replogle suggests car-less, or car-quieted, bicycle routes and other street-engineering improvements serve North Americans' self-interest. Replogle shows the best way to ensure many people will turn to ecologically sustainable alternatives is to reshape communities to make bicycles, buses, and walking the most convenient, pleasant, and cheapest ways to go.

The Gulf War's threat to cheap oil supplies, Replogle says, was another example of how it is in our self-interest to reduce car use and overcome petroleum addiction, including dependence on foreign oil reserves in unstable regions. Per-capita petroleum consumption in U.S. and Canadian cities remains 4.5 times greater than in Europe and 10 times greater than in Japan. Many of North America's competitors produce twice as much output per unit of energy as the United States.

"If we are to enter the 21st century on a path toward sustainable development," Replogle writes, "access to environmentally sustained low-cost means of transportation (such as bicycles and transit) should be established as universal basic human rights in the 1990s. The very future of our planet Earth may depend on our collective success."

At the end of the road, our cars don't necessarily serve our self-interest, or our communities, as well as we thought.✦

Question box

1. Are you happy with your current method of commuting?

2. What would be your dream way of getting around?

3. What are the effects of your mode of travel on the community?

12. Listening

Q: You're discussing politics with friends. One friend doesn't agree with another and calls him a "fascist." Do you suggest he stop the name-calling?

◆◆◆◆◆

Watch out. The "forces" of the politically correct are eyeing us. This "movement" of "nosy Parkers" is conspiring to "regulate everyone's lives." The politically correct are "the new witch hunters" determined to construct a "rigid, paranoid society." They are "thought police" for "the new restrictive order."

At least, that's how a few lengthy magazine articles described the terrifying march of the armies of the politically correct (PC). Trend-spotting journalists use the term to describe holier-than-thou liberals who are convinced they have cornered the market on ethics.

Like most clichés, there is an element of truth in the PC tag: Some liberals (or whatever you want to call them) do act self-righteously. Somehow, however, the magazine writers have overlooked an equally large camp of zealots: politically correct conservatives.

True believers of the far left and far right often serve a useful function in our communities: By polarizing an issue, they can clarify controversies moderates can't quite get around to spelling out in black and white. But, in general, I say a pox on smug extremists of both houses.

People who try to intimidate their opposition into silence deserve to be challenged. Jesus repeatedly rebuked people who judged themselves morally elevated simply because they adhered to the established religious and political doctrine of their time.

The term politically correct first rose up on U.S. campuses in the late 1980s. Initially, it was a self-mocking term used by people who considered themselves progressive. But their opponents soon took over the term, using it to pigeonhole women and minorities who worried college curricula were dominated by Western culture: American history, Greek and Roman philosophy, the Bible, and DWEMs (Dead White European Males, such as Shakespeare, Beethoven, Rousseau, and Adam Smith). Few college courses, said the critics, touched on women's history, ethnic realities, or developing countries.

The definition of politically correct soon broadened like a river in flood. People are now labelled PC if they merely question the status quo: asking why they should inhale someone else's cigarette smoke, why there are homeless in the streets, why food animals should be treated brutally, why a drunk should drive, why a couple should own two cars.

For some reason, the trend-watchers do not judge people as politically correct if they fight for the right to carry guns, vehemently promote free trade, believe women alone should raise children in the home, hate welfare, argue for the end of socialized medicare, or try to ban a children's book because it criticizes logging practices. Both liberals and conservatives are capable of moralistic bullying to silence those who question the status quo.

As put-downs go, "PC" is the virtual equivalent of "right-wing fascist." Unfortunately, those who like to dismiss people by throwing around the PC classification are guilty of exactly what they accuse the PCs of doing. It's called hypocrisy. By name-calling, labelling, and cynically writing off people, discussion is stifled, minds closed, and democracy restricted.

Why not have a reasonable discussion, for example, about whether Shakespeare's *Taming of the Shrew* (a play under attack in some quarters as sexist) reflected a male-dominated culture? Shakespeare, though a breathtaking genius, is not sacred, not above criticism. Why not converse about the ideological shibboleths of both liberals and conservatives, such as whether sexual liberation has led to problems, women should be purposefully promoted in academia and management, marriage is a worthwhile institution, abortion is evil, elementary schools should emphasize the three Rs, some art denigrates women, workers should work harder, and young men should get off welfare? Rather than constantly acting as if it's my-way-or-the-highway, there would be less name-calling, less ideological strong-arming, less pandering to base human instinct — all of which tend to block out a fresh way of seeing the world.

"As a nation, we need to find a basis for diversity other than a multiplicity of separate, hostile communities," says American historian Bruce Schulman, of the University of California in Los Angeles, writing about growing polarization. "We need," he said, "to rebuild a sense of national identity without underestimating human variety."

Instead of yearning for uniformity, we should nurture a truly civil civilization. To put it simply, we could use a little more politeness when we're with people with whom we don't agree.

Some mothers talk about treating all the world's children as if they were their own. Jewish theologian Martin Buber wrote about going beyond seeing the other person as an object, and developing an "I-thou" relationship with him or her. Eighteenth-century philosopher Immanuel Kant spoke of seeing people not as "means," but as "ends in themselves."

A long line of Western philosophers (including many DWEMs) have claimed if people with opposing views open their hearts and minds to truly listen to one another, they will often find themselves integrating conflicting positions and coming up with a more creative solution.

Authentic dialogue is anathema to the dogmatic. And it's not easy for any of us. At the least, it means we have to stop thinking we know what others are going to say before the words actually emerge from their lips.✦

Question box

1. Is it hard for you to calmly listen to someone giving an opposing point of view? Do you find it tempting to label people? (You can admit it, most of us do it.)

2. Can you think of times you've had good discussions with people? Were you able to hear their viewpoint and express yours?

3. What are the effects of dismissing and rejecting people with whom we don't agree?

13. *Affairs of heart/ affairs of state*

Q: You are a politician. You find out an opposing politician, who constantly talks about the importance of family values, had an affair five years ago. Would you leak the news to the media?

◆◆◆◆◆

Just when Gennifer Flowers ran out of dirty things to say and you thought it was safe to watch TV and read newspapers again, a leading British politician was forced to tell the world he once had an extra-marital affair.

Smut-smear stories definitely seem to be a trend. Such an ugly trend that, on most counts, they don't leave room for discussion of subtle ethical points. The supermarket tabloid that paid to have Flowers claim a torrid 12-year affair with Democratic presidential hopeful Bill Clinton acted as outrageously unethical as a newspaper can get, even for a rag that regularly reports on Elvis sightings and humans mating with inter-galactic aliens.

Flowers' accusations only became public after the tabloid offered her tens of thousands of dollars. Any reporter knows a lot of nuts out there will say countless things, virtually anything, for attention. Dangle big money in front of them and the possibilities for flights of fancy skyrocket. Flowers' story, which now-president Clinton denies, was hungrily pounced upon by North American television, and some newspapers, despite failing to meet even rudimentary tests of accuracy, the media's first ethical commitment.

All these recent "sexposés," however, reveal political ethics might be stooping even lower than some journalists' ethics. Many suspect Flowers' allegations against the Democratic party's front-runner were hooked into an organized political smear campaign. In Britain, little doubt exists the leader of the Liberal-Democrat party, Paddy Ashdown, was victimized for political ends. He told the media about his old extra-marital affair with his secretary only after burglars stole the exact file that recounted the brief relationship. Someone had offered to sell the stolen file to the tabloids.

The complicated ethical question raised by these sex stories centers on whether the public deserves to know if politicians have been sexually intimate with people other than their spouses. We can indulge in a smirk over high-profile sexual revelations. But should we care? Is this stuff really important when it comes to making our lives, our communities, more livable?

The standard journalistic rule says politicians' private lives are not relevant unless they somehow negatively affect the way politicians handle the people's business. This principle is not as helpful as it appears.

A few decades ago, journalists interpreted it to mean politicians' sex lives were completely off limits. The Clinton blow-up, as well as the scandal following former Democratic leadership hopeful Gary Hart, show the media have changed its understandings of the rule. "I don't think there is a neat distinction between private and public life," says Wesley Cragg, author of *Contemporary Moral Issues*. "I think the way a politician lives in private is cautiously relevant to the public. Ethics can't be compartmentalized. The question is whether the politician in his private life shows a willingness to exploit individuals."

While liberal individualism promotes the idea what people do in the privacy of their bedrooms is their own business, Cragg opts for what he considers the more conservative belief that a politician's private life reflects on the values he or she brings to community affairs. In ranking the seriousness of different sins politicians can commit, extra-marital affairs sit roughly in the middle, says Richard Wasserstrom, professor of moral philosophy at the University of California, Santa Clara. Law-breaking and financial corruption by politicians is much more worrisome than an affair. Although nobody ever investigated Richard Nixon's sex habits, Cragg says his entire life seemed characterized by dishonesty. To most people, it's clear the Watergate scandal was more morally corrupt than an out-of-bounds love affair.

It would also be more grievous for a politician to beat his wife or children than have an affair, says Wasserstrom. "Abusiveness means you don't care about other people's well-being. It's a big strike against being a good politician," he said in an interview. An ethical offense that would rank as more trivial than an affair includes being rude to people, insensitive to their feelings. And it's ethically irrelevant if a politician approves of masturbation or practices sex in anything other than the missionary position, Wasserstrom says. "This is just table manners." (Often, he says, people mistake religious custom for morality.)

In certain circumstances, there could actually be nothing wrong with an extra-marital affair, says Wasserstrom, who once wrote a widely published scholarly article exploring that idea. Most people marry with the idea they will stay monogamous. "That's one of the ways in which an affair can be judged immoral — if it involves cheating, if it involves breaking promises, if it involves lying. That would seem relevant to public life." But if a couple enters into a relationship after making it clear they might have sexual relationships with other people, Wasserstrom makes a reasonable case that such an affair would not be deceitful or unethical.

Although it might shock some, an above-board extra-marital affair does not necessarily signal an immoral, untrustworthy politician. In Europe, for example, politicians' affairs are treated with tolerant amusement, even admiration. "Perhaps in Europe people don't reasonably expect their spouses won't have an affair," says Wasserstrom. "Then, when they do have an affair, they haven't done anything wrong."

Whatever the circumstances, a politician's sex life should be handled with delicacy by the media. A media outlet's desire to titillate its audience can grievously damage a responsible person's reputation. In a thorough biography of Brian Mulroney, *The Politics of Ambition,* reporter John Sawatsky, a stickler for accuracy, touched on the former Canadian prime minister's past extra-marital affairs — with restraint. The references take up less than a couple of paragraphs in the entire book.

Such Canadian moderation is probably the way to go. The prime minister's reported extra-marital affairs are worth noting, Cragg says, because they support Sawatsky's carefully crafted thesis that Mulroney, despite some positive attributes, is a man obsessed by personal ambition and the need to conquer.

"There's nothing particularly important about sexual relationships, but what you discover in a politician's private life is a pattern that indicates either concern for other people, or callous disregard for them," Cragg says. "Sawatsky was trying to provide a complete portrait of a person who was having a terrific impact on the future of [the] country."✦

1. Have you ever wanted to have an affair outside marriage? Why? How do you feel about it now?

2. Do you think having an affair says anything important about your character or a politician's character?

3. Do you think the media have the right to report politicians' affairs?

4. All in all, do you think the media bind your community together or tear it apart?

14. Medicine: You don't always need what you want

Q: Your 76-year-old mother is extremely ill and incapable of making decisions for herself. A doctor says an experimental, costly operation may give her a chance of surviving about a year longer. Do you agree to the operation?

◆◆◆◆◆

- A man needs his appendix removed.

- Parents want their child immunized against scarlet fever.

- An infertile couple seeks in vitro fertilization.

- The family of an elderly, terminally ill man hope to keep him on life support.

Who deserves medical treatment the most? That question is being asked more often as the fast-rising cost of medical care has grown into the key health issue in North America today. When we recognize our community has financial limits, numerous ethical problems rise up about how to distribute health care justly.

The notion of going without is not well-received in a society in which most of us believe we should get any health care we desire. Still, all of us may have to start talking soon about rationing medicine. "It's becoming the most important problem in health care and bioethics. There never could be enough money to pay all the health care needs of everybody, even in rich countries, let alone poor countries," says John Williams, an ethical consultant for the Canadian Medical Association.

Politicians, health officials, and the public must develop an ethic of scarcity. "The goal is to best serve the common good," says Professor Michael Garland, of the Center for Ethics in Health Care, located in Oregon. The state recently began a novel rationing program to fund health care for 400,000 poor Oregonians, who unlike the majority of Americans, have no private medical insurance.

"The overriding question is 'Are we wasting our resources on trivial health problems?'" says Garland. When someone runs to the emergency ward with the flu or a skin rash, asks for dental X rays every year or demands "unproven" sigmoid screening for colon cancer, Garland believes it's fair to ask whether he or she is being responsible.

Moral transgressions also occur, particularly in the U.S. private health care system, when medical officials over-use questionable medical procedures to hike profits. When Garland's son recently broke his arm, the boy went to a U.S. hospital, which wanted him to stay three days. Garland believes only one was necessary.

If money is wasted on frivolous health care, it hurts support for more important medical procedures in our communities. It also cuts into spending on society-supported programs such as education and social services. Canada has nationalized health care, and in principle it is available on an equal basis to those in need. The U.S. health system, built around private insurance, provides patients with the treatment each can afford. Still, Garland says citizens of both countries bring similar "blank check" or "credit card" attitudes to doctors and hospitals. That attitude, in conjunction with an aging population and shiny new, hyper-expensive medical technology, has caused health-care costs to skyrocket.

In the past, the burden of deciding how much care to provide patients has mainly gone to the providers: doctors, nurses, and hospital staff. And providers disagree over how to act out their commitment to give patients good medical care. "Some doctors think cost should be no object — they're supposed to provide the best health care possible," says Williams. These doctors, he says, hold to the idea that the only thing that counts is the patient-doctor relationship.

But cost-conscious doctors take into account the community — especially its financial resources. They tell a patient an expensive treatment will likely do them little, or no, good. Ethically, Williams believes the frugal approach is superior.

To determine how health care would be provided for the poor in Oregon, officials followed the public's opinion on which treatments were most, and least, important to fund. Following what Garland calls "a community sense of self-control," Oregon set up a system called Medicaid that pays for most medical treatments for poor people, except those treatments low on the medical pecking order. At the top of Oregon's list of critical treatments are things such as repairing open neck wounds, appendectomies, care for pregnant women, treatment for low birth-weight babies, and therapy for meningitis. Preventive medicine ranked highly, including screening for hearing problems, teeth cleaning, contraception management, immunizations, and mammograms. Comfort care for the dying, too, was judged crucial.

Oregon's Medicaid system, however, will not cover treatment for things such as acne, varicose veins, or life-support for babies born without brains. In vitro fertilization, which is costly and often fails, will not be funded. Oregon officials will also overrule financing liver transplants for chronic alcoholics who have damaged their internal organs. "We're trying to exercise some social wisdom. The focus is effective care, rather than long-shot care," says Garland.

The cost of caring for the terminally ill or aged, who have little chance of long-term recovery, makes up a large part of the scarcity debate. More than 40% of Canada's health-care spending is directed toward the final hospital stay before death, according to studies, says George McLauchlin, an official with McMaster University's Faculty of Health Sciences. "It's a staggering waste, in some respects, of scarce social resources."

Much questionable spending flows from society trying to avoid "the inevitability of death," says Williams. Although it's important not to begrudge elderly people good medical care, Williams believes the elderly should write "living wills" that would help their loved ones determine when to pull the plug on life support. Why perform extraordinary, and expensive, operations just to extend a terminal patient's life a few months or weeks?

Oregon's medical ranking system has merit, says Williams, but it falls short on some ethical counts. First, it is not egalitarian, like Canada's medicare system, because rationing applies only to the poor. And by completely eliminating some care options, the Oregon system doesn't have the flexibility of medicare. In Canada, waiting lists for certain procedures provide a better form of rationing, he says. Those people whose health is most in danger receive an operation first.

The American sense of justice, he says, only ensures the right of an individual to do as he or she pleases with his or her money. Canada's nationalized health care system links justice to equality. Williams believes that works out better both economically and ethically.

Where to begin keeping costs under control? Williams would start simply with public education programs to teach everyone — from medical students to patients to doctors — about the financial waste involved in things such as unnecessary Caesarean sections, useless heart bypass operations, too-long hospital stays, and the over-prescription of drugs and medical testing.

Something must be done to stop health-care costs from rising above the current 12% of the GNP in the United States, and 9% of the GNP in Canada. In an era where everyone is increasingly concerned about rising government spending, politicians, health officials, and patients — all of us — must make better decisions about where to spend our health-care money. ✦

Question box

1. When you or your loved ones seem sick, do you rush immediately to a doctor or an emergency ward?

2. Have doctors ever given you treatment or pills you found out were probably unnecessary?
   How does your community lose when such waste occurs?

3. Would you be willing to support a health-care system that refused to fund certain medical treatments, or drugs, considered long-shot?

15. *Paying your fair share*

Q: A carpenter does a $1,500 renovation on your home. He'll charge you $250 less if you pay him in cash, so he can avoid paying taxes on the job. Do you?

◆◆◆◆◆

In these days, when mistrust of politicians is growing, it will probably turn out be controversial to speak out about how important it is to pay taxes. A long-time vexation sparks this defense of paying one's fair share into the public purse: the Fraser Institute's famous Tax Freedom Day, which for more than a decade has been announced with much fanfare each June across the land in Canada.

Tax Freedom Day marks the mythical time of year the free-enterprise lobby group estimates we've finally paid all our taxes and so from now until December, "We're working for ourselves!" Hallelujah. The media typically react to Tax Freedom Day with horrified gee-whizzes and cynicism about government. The public shakes its head in frustrated amazement — thinking bureaucrats are solely dedicated to ripping hard-earned dollars out of innocent hands.

Tax Freedom Day is a clever, effective public-relations trick. In many ways, however, it's a lie.

Don't think I'm not bothered by taxes. I feel the same knot in the stomach most do when store clerks punch the register's sales-tax button. And April nights spent calculating my income tax have caused more than a few rushes to the cookie jar for comfort food. As it was said in *Gone With the Wind,* "Death and taxes and childbirth — there's never any convenient time for any of them."

I'm also concerned about waste in government: The $1,600-a-night hotel rooms for federal politicians, and any senior civil servant who believes public life is an endless gravy train rather than an opportunity to better society. Still, such criticisms of government don't stop me feeling offended by the simplistic, lop-sided message of Tax Freedom Day, which the corporate-backed Fraser Institute invented to convince people governments overspend.

The most troubling deception of Tax Freedom Day is its catch-phrase, when the head of the Fraser Institute, Michael Walker, intones each year: "Tax Freedom Day is, effectively, the day when the average family starts working for itself."

This bit of Madison Avenue gimmickry implies taxes are nothing more than a parasitic drain on hard-slogging Canadians and Americans. Pushed by the likes of the Fraser Institute, corporations, and many media, this has become the wisdom of the streets, bars, and squash courts.

But the Fraser Institute conveniently ignores how taxes finance services that help all of us. In other words, when I pay taxes, I am working for myself and my family. The vast majority of us benefit greatly, at one time or another, from taxes.

We learned how to read and multiply and prepare for jobs at taxpayer-funded schools, colleges, and universities. Our loved ones have had mental and physical problems treated by publicly financed doctors, nurses, and psychiatrists. We feel relieved when the police respond to our 911 call. Traffic lights ($50,000 for each intersection) help my car avoid crashing into yours. Children kick soccer balls on taxpayer-supported fields. And I dare anyone to claim they haven't had a close relative who hasn't had to rely at some time on unemployment insurance or perhaps welfare. "Taxes," said the famous turn-of-the-century lawyer, Oliver Wendell Holmes, "are what we pay for a civilized society."

By making it seem taxes do not benefit all, the Fraser Institute is promoting the dubious ethics of radical individualism. By celebrating the illusory day "we begin working for ourselves," Tax Freedom Day implies the only thing that counts is individuals, and perhaps, their immediate families. Society, in other words our neighbors, doesn't count. The Fraser Institute does not take seriously that we're all interconnected. In its small universe, things such as contributing to the common good through taxes are not valued. It's us against them.

Don't get me wrong. I'm as much a fan of the market system as anyone. The market can be highly productive, efficient, and responsive to public needs and desires. It can also be capricious and brutal. It needs to be balanced by public institutions. Even business needs government. True-believing free-marketers should stop trying to ignore that all economies rely on taxpayers' dollars. Where would manufacturers be, for example, without government-financed roads and bridges to get their product to customers?

One of the numerous pitfalls of blindly celebrating "the day we start working for ourselves" is it threatens democratic institutions. If people think governments exist merely to steal half their salaries, they grow disdainful. If they succumb to pure cynicism about government, then they're more inclined to stop voting, stop volunteering for political parties, stop studying issues in their complexity, stop believing it's possible to work for change (including better ways to spend public money). When we cease to believe government is part of us, some will also find it easier to rationalize the artful tax dodge. As Plato, the influential Greek philosopher figured out way back in the fifth century B.C., "When there is an income tax, the just man will pay more and the unjust less on the same amount of income."

Ironically, even the Fraser Institute recognizes people who grow furious about taxes will be less inclined to pay up. They'll also be more likely to tunnel into an underground economy. A few years ago, Walker estimated Canada's underground, often-illegal economy, was growing so fast it was worth more than $80 billion a year. If the underground economy was taxed at the current rate, Walker said it would pay off all federal and provincial deficits. It's strange the Fraser Institute continues to encourage people to despise handing over their taxes, given such destructive side-effects.

The less people and corporations pay their fair share to government, the more those who dutifully send in their income tax checks and pay sales taxes must carry the free-loaders — those clever tax-evaders who don't seem to mind other working people paying to educate their children, take care of their aging parents, and protect them from all those things that go bump in the night.✦

Question box

1. What benefits have you and your family received from taxpayer-funded services?

2. Is our financial responsibility primarily to ourselves and our family? What responsibility, if any, do we have to our community?

3. What kind of society would we have without taxation?

---

16. Good neighbors

Q: You are exhausted and just want to watch a video. Friends need someone to babysit their child so they can attend a school meeting. Do you sit for them?

◆◆◆◆◆

In a movie about a big-city cop who hides in an Amish commune to protect a boy who's seen a murder, something surprising takes place in what would otherwise be just another thriller. An achingly moving scene points to a hole in the heart of North America.

As the loner detective in *Witness* settles deeper into the Amish lifestyle, he takes part in a customary barn-raising, joining dozens of bearded men, plus women and children, in raising a magnificent wooden structure against the pure-blue sky. By the time the sun sets, one more Amish family has a barn and the detective (played by Harrison Ford) realizes the community's ethic of mutual responsibility provides a feeling of belonging he's never experienced in the rat-eat-rat world outside.

"In the spirit of the pioneer's 'house raising,' lies the salvation of the republic," wrote Frederick Jackson Turner. The historian was talking about overcoming the problems of turn-of-the-century North America. But Turner could have been talking about contemporary times. These days we seem to be obsessed about individual rights and freedoms, forgetting about helping each other: about our responsibility to community, country, and the environment.

We're all busy these days invoking our constitutional rights as we square off on every conceivable topic: right to avoid wearing seat belts, right to die, right to abortion, right to disseminate racist literature, right to refuse blood transfusions, right to pray in school, right to any health care we want, right to join a male sports team, right to wear a religious turban, right to refuse breathalyzer tests, right to shop on Sundays, right to be drunk in a public place, and right to carry a gun.

Most of us have become experts at arguing for rights for blacks, Indians, women, Hispanics, Quebecois, students, business owners, workers, and people with disabilities. But have we pushed rights talk about as far as it should go? It seems to be hampering our ability to talk about obligations. Neither the rigorous Amish lifestyle, nor their watch-out-for-one-another attitude, are considered hip in these days of do your own thing.

We have charters and bills of rights, but few people are calling for a charter of responsibilities:

- Millions don't bother to vote.

- Fathers take off on their children.

- Offspring ignore aging parents.

- Teenagers think liberty means license to a car, to engage in sex, to consume alcohol.

- Regional governments cry for more powers from central governments.

- People drop out of church, sports, and volunteer groups.

- Programs for the needy grow weak.

Civic virtue, the glue that holds our nations together, sometimes seems to be losing its grip in our individualistic, consumer culture. "I think the values of the marketplace have infiltrated every institution in Canada family, the church, the legal system," says Arthur Schafer, head of Canada's Centre for Professional and Applied Ethics. "Anti-human, commercial values are dominating many spheres of life. It would be surprising if the family and everything else weren't affected. How can I be a competitive, individualistic, gratification-maximizer at school and at work and become a generous, altruistic, self-sacrificing person at home?"

Rising fears — real and imagined — are contributing to many looking out only for Number One. "Now that we're coming into economic hard times, I think the sense of each man for himself, save your own skin, get whatever advantage you can, may sink public spiritedness and make it so much more difficult to preserve our sense of obligation to community. Each of us is saying, 'Give me, Give me, Give me' — because we're afraid. We're afraid no one's going to look out for us."

Cross-border shopping, for example, drives home the destructive effects of both self-interest and free trade's push to "duty-free" borders (another revealing term). In countries where wages are more meager and taxes lower because fewer services are provided, things such as gas, shoes, food, and appliances often cost less. But tens of thousands of jobs are being lost because hordes of Canadians and Americans won't say no to alleged bargains in adjoining countries. "This is each individual demanding the liberty to buy goods at a lower price," says Schafer. "The result is a kind of freeloading."

It's the conflict, says Schafer, between a person's right to buy in the marketplace where it's cheapest and a person's sense of community responsibility, which says: "If I exercise that right, my neighbors are going to be laid off, maybe even I will be laid off."

North Americans' shifting values reveal how they're running away from responsibility, says the author of *Fragmented Gods*, Reginald Bibby. His public-opinion surveys reveal a big contradiction: The vast majority of people tell pollsters the thing they most strongly value is a good relationship. But far fewer care about "concern for others" and "generosity," the qualities that make a relationship work.

Signs of hope?

Ironically, like the widespread poverty created by the 1930s Depression, environmental destruction makes it acceptable to talk again about caring for something other than oneself: in this case, the earth, and by extension, all of us.

Recent polls show four out of five North Americans are willing to accept a lower standard of living to protect the environment. People seem ready to give up the right to wasteful consumption for the sake of a higher quality of life. It could be a hint we're beginning to recognize we're all in this together: societal problems require a team effort.

Politicians should be leading us to show greater responsibility, but Schafer says most don't have the courage. Even John F. Kennedy initially took flak for his famous: "Ask not what your country can do for you, ask what you can do for your country." Education is one way to encourage voluntary civic virtue to flower naturally. But Schafer says incentives, disincentives, and straight-ahead coercive laws — democratically agreed upon — may also be necessary.

By balancing rights with responsibility, our mass society still will not end up as close as an Amish commune. But keeping the balance between freedom and duty is necessary to stop our fragile communities from spinning apart.

As Benjamin Barber, the American author of *Strong Democracy*, says: "Liberty isn't free. It's paid for in the currency of obligation." ✦

Question box

1. How much are you involved in your community?
    Do you think the glue that keeps community together
    is coming unstuck?

2. Do you think you are more concerned about your
    rights, or your responsibilities? Which ones?

3. Would you accept a moderately lower standard of
    living to protect the jobs of your neighbors or to
    protect the environment?

Part 3
Working it out in the workplace

There are people who have money and people who are rich.

Coco Chanel

◆◆◆◆◆

The love of money, as the saying goes, is the root of all evil. But right now most of us rely on jobs and the market economy to keep us fed, clothed, and housed. Money makes our communities go round. Maybe we can play the money game by rules that allow us to make a living, produce something of value, and maximize everyone's enjoyment.◆

17. Balancing competition with cooperation

Q: While he's drunk, a friend tells you an important trade secret about his company. Your company could profit if it took advantage of the information. What do you do?

◆◆◆◆◆

The shark's teeth look more menacing than switchblades. The beast's dirty gray hulk swims through the telephone company's TV commercial like an icon of death — instilling horrifying fear of The Competitor. Life is tough, says the commercial's message. Keep on your guard. One false move and your business, your livelihood, and your self-worth will be gobbled up by corporate predators like an innocent fish.

The telephone company's ad campaign creates a dangerously misleading impression about business and life, says Michael McDonald, founder of the Canadian Business and Professional Ethics Network. Unfortunately, those most inexperienced with the real world are most likely to believe the campaign's life-is-vicious philosophy, particularly students who McDonald says have a "romantic, exaggerated view of how important it is just to look after themselves alone."

When to compete, when to cooperate? Young people, especially business students, overrate the value of a competitive drive in achieving personal success, McDonald says. They underrate business' desire for team players — employees who will look out for the interests of the company. If a company needs to build a bridge, for example, it needs cooperators, not competitors. Owners fear staff members who are eager to cut each others' throats. Most enterprises rely for long-run success on loyal relationships with employees, customers, suppliers and even other companies. "Today's competitor," McDonald says, "might be tomorrow's partner."

There's no doubt North American capitalism is generally based on competition. But rivalry has become such a dominant metaphor for our culture that many don't realize how much collaboration makes it go round. There are a lot of people not in a position to compete in our society — small children, the very old, those who are otherwise dependent, McDonald says. "There are an enormous number of rich relationships in which competition would be wrong."

Competition is not right in a family, between spouses, between parent and child, or between siblings, McDonald says. "It's not a good way to make kids into strong, healthy adults."

Competition is often not good for community life. There's little place for competition in the many non-profit societies, churches, or social causes we support. And take traffic. When McDonald catches himself racing other motorists on his daily commute to his university, he realizes he's been tricked into unhealthy competing. "The whole point of our traffic system is safety."

Ironically, sometimes competition is not even best in that sphere which we believe exemplifies it: sports. There's not only a baseball team's obvious need for collaboration. Susan Butt, author of *The Psychology of Sport,* says individual-oriented sports can suffer without it. Canada's national ski team, she says, has performed poorly at times because members wouldn't help each other.

And is competition as necessary as many seem to think in schools — where more than a few parents argue that As and Fs are essential to motivating children? It seems that instilling a love of learning, for its own sake, would provide more solid, longer-term motivation. Although McDonald says it's fine for academics to bolster their ego by competing with colleagues, he personally doesn't like it. In his own field of philosophy, he welcomes women who have recently questioned the "macho" tradition of debate, which uses the language of combat to describe "overcoming," "defeating," and "beating" opponents. Platonic dialogues offer one alternative, McDonald says; they are not competitive, but a collaborative process designed to best discern the truth. Although combative intellectual debate can be exciting for those who are up to it, the drawback is that it frightens many students. They then lose out on the insights offered by philosophy — the same way children intimidated by one-upping young athletes lose out on the benefits of sport.

It is even more important to closely analyze competition in the economic sphere. Competitive capitalism (balanced in our mixed economy by government intervention) determines almost everything about our Western way of life: jobs, lifestyles, environment, and children's futures.

Thoughtful people in business don't ignore the ramifications of competition. McDonald often talks with CEOs who believe that deception and lack of cooperation are inevitable in business. Nevertheless, the CEOs feel moral qualms about participating in it.

To judge whether business is ethical, McDonald says it's worthwhile to compare it to a game. The rules of business, he says, are provided by the law, professional disciplinary bodies, individual consciences, whistle-blowers, and the media.

It does not break the rules of business to mislead competitors, McDonald says. But it does break the rules to abuse the trust of a friend. Friends in business have to be careful to clarify with each other when they're competing and when they're not.

Though McDonald says it is perfectly acceptable to beat a competing company at providing consumers with the highest-quality, cheapest widgets in town, the goal of the game of business, unlike war, should never descend to humiliating opponents.

He justifies economic competition by saying it makes our lives easier; it pushes companies to produce more goods at lower prices. While competition makes some winners rich, McDonald suggests it can be an effective way to "distribute excess wealth — beyond the amount that's necessary for human survival and dignity."

One of the toughest questions raised by business competition concerns what happens to "innocent bystanders." We can't deny people suffer as a result of competitive economics. Yet, McDonald says, everyone who loses in business, such as a person who makes a bad investment, is not necessarily a victim. He doesn't automatically endorse government intervention to stave off bankruptcies or save laid-off workers. Such moves can often be more trouble than they're worth.

If we care about human dignity, however, the often-harsh realities of competitive economics have to be offset by other values. "If you just say, 'We live in a competitive marketplace, so some people are just going to have to go hungry, kids will have to be malnourished,' you really should start questioning your reasons for saying that," McDonald says. "I don't think we should just say: 'That's what happens to the losers in society. Their lives go down the tube, their families go down the tube. Tough luck.'"✦

Question box

1. What do you feel are the main values of the marketplace?

2. How do you think we could teach fair competition and cooperation in schools, professions, and business?

---

18. Are you serving others, or yourself?

Q: You are a waiter. You know you will get a huge tip from one table if you show it undivided attention. You're not sure what tip to expect from other tables. What do you do?

✦✦✦✦✦

- A doctor orders a Caesarean section for a pregnant woman because it's more convenient for his schedule.

- A reporter writes a positive article about a company because she's invested money in it.

- A cabinet minister funnels a large government grant to a friend because she needs to return a favor.

- A Third World leader stays in power because he can amass a personal fortune with taxpayers' money.

The fictional people above all failed the test when faced with a morally charged conflict of interest. Although the stakes vary dramatically, they abrogate trust placed in them; instead of impartially serving the public, they serve themselves.

At first glance, conflict of interest might not seem as clear-cut a wrong as robbing a bank. But some specialists in ethics believe it is potentially far more damaging to modern society. "Conflict of interest does not appear to hurt directly. But it hurts because we set up false advertising about the way the world is run," says Professor Mark Wexler, a widely published ethicist from Simon Fraser University who has been a consultant to many companies. "Straight law-breaking is not conflict of interest. Conflict of interest is the masquerading of truth. It's the essence of corruption. People are queuing in good faith and they're not getting served."

Conflict of interest occurs more often now because our society is becoming increasingly more complex, competitive, and service based. Although the most high-profile cases occur in politics, conflict of interest has the potential to undermine our entire social system.

We trust someone to look after our interests every time we sign up for a professor's course and expect to be marked fairly, not based on whether we sleep with him or her. We assume a police officer will charge a drunk driver, even if the culprit is a fellow police officer. We hire an insurance agent to provide the best way to protect our family's future, not to pick the contract that will give the agent top commission.

The higher someone ranks in society, the more potential for conflict of interest. Workers at a Burger King restaurant have little room to pursue personal interests on the job because they must produce a standard hamburger for a set price. But professionals such as doctors, business people, journalists, and lawyers have greater latitude and thus greater potential to line their own pockets while pretending to serve the public. "The higher up you go, the more discretion you have and the more you have to show impartiality," says Wexler. "You can't just be favoring yourself or your friends."

Conflict of interest dilemmas flow in part out of clashing ideologies, says Wexler. Economist Adam Smith taught that the aim of Western capitalism is to maximize profit, "but the physician is not supposed to be maximizing the number of patients he's seeing."

The really high-profile conflicts of interest occur in politics. Ethics specialist Paul Russell believes that's partly because Western democracy is founded on the principle of trust. The liberal democratic philosophy espoused by John Locke taught that our society can function properly only when public officials always act for the public good.

While some politicians and economists are urging more deregulation and privatization to free up the marketplace, the ethicists believe our complex society, with its growing potential for conflict of interest, needs more regulations, not fewer. As someone said: "Freedom for the shark can mean death for the minnows."

Bureaucracies and companies need more explicit rules on conflict of interest. Governments all over the world should offer more open access to information and set up independent bodies of professionals to establish conflict-of-interest guidelines. Universities, colleges, and high schools should also bring in courses to develop character ethics, says Wexler. People are being trained in job skills for the marketplace. But they're not learning how to resist temptation. They're not learning how to be.✦

Question box

1. Can you think of a conflict of interest you've been in?

2. It's common for people to say mistrust is growing these days. Have you found that true in your life, among the people you know?

3. What would you like to see happen to curtail conflict of interest in society?
   Would you accept more regulations?

19. *Keeping the code*

Q: You're a police officer sworn to protect the public. You've been assigned to arrest people blocking women from entering an abortion clinic. But
your religious principles say abortion is murder. Do you adhere to your professional oath?

◆◆◆◆◆

Dr. Charlotte Waddell was among the five students who did
not stand up when the Hippocratic oath was recited at her
graduation ceremony. The group of five soon-to-be blessed
physicians, solid students who'd taken leadership roles during their medical training, had debated with the rest of their
class whether to follow medical tradition and recite the famous oath.

When the majority of grads in the faculty of health sciences at McMaster University in Hamilton voted to swear to
an abridged version of the oath, the five dissented. They had
too many reservations about the ancient Greek medical ethics
code. They wanted to recite a code they actually believed in.

A lot of professional ethicists think codes of conduct are
becoming more and more essential in the workplace. The
Hippocratic Oath is a good example of a bad one. Credited to
a semi-mythical physician from 400 B.C., it is a moral mine
field. Yet it's still recited, in various versions, at graduation
ceremonies at most medical schools. Waddell and her colleagues are not the first to protest it. While the Hippocratic
oath's general recommendation that physicians put the health

of their patients first is often cited as a near-sacred principle, the oath contains a surprising number of philosophical pitfalls.

The standard oath condemns abortion and seems to ban euthanasia. It also stresses curing disease rather than preventing it, and some translations emphasize physicians' right to personal prosperity. "I felt regret we couldn't come up with an oath — perhaps by writing it ourselves — that was more contemporary, yet still had deep meaning," says Waddell.

The Hippocratic oath runs the danger of turning many North American physicians into hypocrites. Most schools require grads to swear to the code even though most don't believe it. Thousands of Canadian and U.S. physicians, trained at schools using the oath, break it by performing abortions. The oath also appears to condemn mercy killing, even though many physicians (and the majority of North Americans, according to opinion polls) support euthanasia. The Hippocratic oath shuts down dialogue on complex ethical issues that are worthy of intense scrutiny. Or it's so vague as to be virtually meaningless.

Oaths are important, Waddell says. Physicians, like people in other vocations, need one that is significant. "The Hippocratic Oath is more an icon than a useful guide for moral reflection," agrees Seattle Professor David Zimmerman, who specializes in medical ethics. "There are no arguments in it. It assumes the answer already. It closes questions that should be open morally. In other cases, it's just vague and begs the question."

Oaths are valuable for any professionals, whether they're accountants, engineers, lawyers, teachers, or journalists. People practicing a craft in which they carry responsibility for others can benefit from ethical guidelines based on clear arguments. Medical ethicist Alister Browne, however, thinks most physicians treat the Hippocratic oath the way some couples treat orthodox marriage vows that refer to remaining together until death — as a somewhat strange tradition not to be taken seriously.

But why should any people today, including couples and new citizens of a country, take oaths they don't really intend to follow?

Throughout history, vows have meant something. If they are recited merely out of loyalty to tradition, they become a mockery. Empty oaths can contribute to empty lives; they don't lead to strengthening of character. If an oath contains values with which those taking it can't agree, the oath should be transformed so that it can be recited with pride and commitment.◆

Question box

1. Have you ever recited an oath that is important to you? Is it still important?

2. How should we establish strong codes of conduct for married people, new citizens, people testifying in court, and professionals such as journalists, lawyers, and engineers?

20. *No one owns the land*

Q: Your company is harming the environment. If you tell authorities, your company could go down the tubes. You need your job. Do you keep silent?

◆◆◆◆◆

From mountaintop to mountaintop, as far as young Bart van der Kamp could see, towered Douglas fir trees of monumental proportions. It was 1961. The primeval forest that stretched out before van der Kamp was filled with other-worldly trees, with trunks thicker than Parthenon pillars. They overwhelmed the senses.

The west coast of North America was once dominated by such myth-inspiring trees. Little remains. "It's pretty sad," says van der Kamp, 50, a professor of forestry science in Canada. "The most magnificent types of old growth are all gone. They just don't exist any more." After a lifetime of forestry research, van der Kamp suggested North America's virgin forests, and the sustainability of the ranges that remain, have been sacrificed to greed.

Forestry, in many ways, is the most important business-environmental issue in many parts of the continent. Logging the forest has contributed to the well-being of millions of people by providing taxes and hundreds of thousands of jobs. But now hikers, natives, fly-fishers, environmentalists, cruise-ship operators, skiers, game wardens, campers, and tourists are insisting on having a say in what kind of values will be brought to handling the forest.

Forestry is a prominent example of an industry that needs a new code of ethics to help it come to terms with a new problem: ecological destruction. Moral pressure is coming not only from outside the industry, but from within.

After decades of putting up with the "very conservative, very industry-oriented bias" of the forestry faculty at his west coast university, student Peter Opie is one of many who lobbied to get the faculty to look beyond seeing the forest only as an economic resource. His group, Students for Forestry Awareness, ventured into new territory by bringing together foresters, environmentalists, and ethicists for a conference.

With many voices calling to be heard, a big question in forestry ethics revolves around who the forests are for. It is a question that can be asked of any business that relies on natural resources for its livelihood — mining, fishing, farming, even tourism. Many people studying forestry practices have stated the beneficiaries of the forests should be all the people of the related region through successive generations.

Though such a statement rightfully recognizes that present and future generations have a huge stake in the forests, it's too restrictive, says ethicist Michael McDonald. It leaves out people who don't live in the region, as well as animals and plants. Critics who describe North American rain forests as the "Brazil of North America," McDonald suggests, believe the rapid destruction of our forests could be as harmful to the planet as burning the South American jungle to make way for cattle ranching.

Everything is inter-connected in the environment. Clearcut logging eliminates animal and plant species, reducing the world's biological diversity, says James Coufal, an ethicist at the State University of New York, Syracuse. Many scientists believe excessive logging contributes to potentially devastating global warming by dangerously increasing CO_2 levels in the atmosphere. Our continent's lush forests turn out to be both a blessing for citizens and a responsibility.

Philosophically, van der Kamp finds himself between those who say a "tree is such a holy organ we have no right to chop it down" and forest companies who "only see dollar signs standing on stumps." Justification is required every time someone chain saws a tree, says van der Kamp. If a tree dies to make a piano, van der Kamp thinks that's fine. If it falls just to make a profit or preserve a job, that's no longer enough for him.

The biggest, best trees in North America, and the world, are already gone, says van der Kamp. Efforts to save remaining parcels of old-growth forest are worthwhile, but it's a little late already. Now we need to emphasize sustainability. Although some radical ecologists assume the forests are destroyed the moment humans touch them, van der Kamp believes nature can be "a place where humans both live and work."

He's seen Swedish forests that have been used by humans for 300 years and are still "beautiful places to be." But in North American forests, humans haven't served either the industry or themselves well. Our logging towns will soon be dying because we've failed to maintain the forests' productive capacity — an environmental ethic that van der Kamp, a Christian, says was spelled out eons ago in the Book of Genesis.

Government forest policy has often encouraged companies to compete destructively for the same piece of forest, leading to "the tragedy of the commons," where land is pillaged because no one in particular has responsibility for it. With globalization of markets, van der Kamp also sees tremendous pressure on forest companies to take as much from the forests as fast as they can, then run. The corporations move on to other countries or other lines of business altogether.

The quick-profit motive has caused unfortunate things to happen to responsible forest companies that invested in forests' future through prudent logging and silviculture. Because responsible practices marginally reduced short-term profitability and share value, the companies became vulnerable to corporations bent on hostile take-overs — companies that could care less about sustainability.

And although the rate of tree harvesting has been controlled somewhat by governments, cynically slipshod logging practices have been all too common. The land has been battered. When heavy-logging machines crash over the terrain, the soil compacts in harmful ways that can last a century, van der Kamp says. Rapacious clear-cut logging can also cause mountainsides to wash away, not only hurting fish-spawning streams, but making successful replanting unlikely.

The ultimate goal of those who use the forests should be to maintain "the tapestry" of the land, says Coufal, who is a forester as well as a philosopher. That means taking into account the forest's artistic and esthetic worth. "I believe that the tapestry we weave must be one of demonstrated exemplary stewardship, woven in full concert with all of those neighbors, human and other, who share the loom."

At the policy level, better environmental laws are needed to protect North America's forests, as well as those in Brazil. International laws will help curtail the rape-and-run mentality of irresponsible multi-national logging companies.

At the philosophical level, van der Kamp suggests people need to learn that "to be truly human is to be to some extent sacrificial — that means giving up what you might have in order to allow others, including other species, to survive."

Neither the forestry nor mining companies, the state, nor the citizens of any region own the forests. Van der Kamp thinks humans are "stewards" of the land on behalf of God. The stewardship model also works well for secular environmentalists, including Coufal. Secular stewardship states humans are only "custodians" of the forests.

"At an existential level," says Coufal, "we have to answer to our consciences, fellow humans beings, and those who come after us." ✦

1. Have your views about the need to balance business and the environment changed in recent years? How?

2. What do you think of the idea of making personal sacrifices to protect the environment?

21. *We are what we produce*

Q: You walk into a banquet. You can either sit at a table of well-off business people, or a table of carpenters. Where do you go?

✦✦✦✦✦

"Other people can talk about how to expand the destiny of mankind. I just want to talk about how to fix a motorcycle. I think what I have to say has more value," Robert Pirsig wrote in *Zen and the Art of Motorcycle Maintenance.* In his offbeat 1970s bestseller, Pirsig riveted our attention with long, loving descriptions about repairing his motorcycle.

Linking metaphysics and technology, he told us about a motorcycle trip across North America that punctured the stereotype that mechanical work is done with one's hands. He devoted chapter after chapter to detailing how fixing a lugging engine, fine-tuning an elaborate network of steel and energy, amounts to an intellectual exercise, mastered only with a mind as sharp as a glass cutter.

Performing virtually any skilled trade not only requires a knack for puzzle-solving, but a kind of inner mental calm. In their work, mechanics can embody an elusive transcendent constant Pirsig called Quality, which he believed to be the source of creativity. *Zen and the Art of Motorcycle Maintenance* has sold like crazy on campuses, which is a good thing. Colleges and universities, which idolize disembodied head work, are notorious for ignoring the value of the trades.

It's disturbing that the skilled men and women who have built our physical world — who produce the furniture, condos, jewelry, suits, boats, and cars we strive to obtain — should have to endure low status. Yet television continues to pour out copious images of glamorous, high-flying business people and professionals, while virtually ignoring tradespeople. Even smart sit-coms such as *Murphy Brown* and *Home Improvement* caricature tradespeople as likable goofs.

In schools, young people inhabit a chalk-board world where virtually every adult has been to university. Students can't model themselves after tradespeople because few get on to school property, except to put ladders in students' way. Worse yet, young people who either can't, or don't want to, keep up with English, history, and chemistry are systematically slipped into the vocational stream, giving the impression that's where the slow-folk swim — or often sink. Without really knowing it, we've become hellishly effective at denigrating such things as cement masonry, ironwork, glazing, meat cutting, upholstery, sprinkler-fitting, boilermaking, electricity, horticulture, cable-splicing, printing, cooking, plumbing, engraving, tool-and-die making, pile driving, sail making, refrigeration, floristry, baking, millwrighting, and motorcycle repair.

A counselor at a trades school, Kate Pelletier, says the image of tradespeople as dummies is a big problem. Although a few signs point to the standing of North American tradespeople climbing a little closer to that of their European counterparts, the stigma in North America against the trades can still be irrational. "When I was in high school, we wouldn't even walk down into the vocational wing," says Pelletier. "I don't know what we thought would happen."

The turn-of-the-century American economist who coined the phrase, "conspicuous consumption," hammered together a provocative theory about why we denigrate tradespeople and aggrandize business leaders. In *The Theory of the Leisure*

Class, Thorstein Veblen said industrialized Westerners admire and fear the leisure class the way primitive societies once admired their warriors and hunters. "As Veblen put it, the one with the most scalps hanging from his teepee would gain the most respect. In a modern business era, that same respect is devoted to those who demonstrate conspicuous consumption and leisure — because that means they have wealth without having to work for it," says economist John Sayer.

"Those who have to work for what they earn are not considered successful warriors and hunters, therefore they do not command admiration and fear. The fear comes from the mystique of how the person who has wealth and leisure got it. He didn't get it through work, so he must have got it through some sort of mental process that is not possessed by everybody."

Ironically, Veblen says industrial workers are handed an inferior standing in society even though they cooperate to perform useful work, while corporate bosses are lauded for merely trying to make themselves money.

Skilled tradespeople, who make up roughly 10% of the North American workforce, may have taken their lack of prestige to heart, according to a recent study. A survey by the University of Guelph in Ontario showed, paradoxically, that while most tradespeople feel satisfied with their work and wages, they aren't too sure they want their own children taking up a trade.

"People in the trades are very humble people," said Kate Braid, a licensed carpenter who has written a book about her work, called *Covering Rough Ground*. Although skilled tradespeople possess quiet pride and generally know their work requires ingenuity, math skills, and responsibility, Braid thinks many insecurely put doctors, lawyers, and business people on pedestals.

While Veblen's grand theory still seems to echo in society, something more simple might also help explain the trades low ranking: dirt. Unlike North American tradespeople, Europeans counteract their vocations' grubby image by going well-dressed to work, often in jacket and tie, then changing and showering in immaculate trailers, sometimes with curtains and flower boxes.

As well, the often-times oppressive macho atmosphere pervading North American trades (not to mention business) seems to be fading. Canadian trades now have more women, more people with university backgrounds, and less narrow notions about manhood, says Braid, who also has a masters degree.

Although Peter Norris, an official with the Carpenters' Union, had solid marks at university, he just didn't get off on the hallowed halls. He decided to build on his childhood affection for making things and took up hammer, drill, and power-saw. There is something pure and unambiguous about hanging a door, says Norris. "It is incontrovertibly good."

That's not a claim you can always make about the tasks performed by lawyers, sales agents, stock brokers, or journalists. "The rewards of building things are very real," says Norris, who remains a copious reader with more than 1,000 books at his home. "I still drive by the house I built for my mother and feel satisfaction. My mother was so proud her son could do that."

Tradespeople don't shuffle paper, buy out companies, sell things people don't need, win lawsuits in court, sit around collecting checks from tenants, or watching stock portfolios fluctuate. They produce. Yet, while it would be cheap to start casting easy aspersions at investors or the desk-bound, it's been just fine to belittle or ignore the handiwork of people such as Braid, who has worked on dozens of highrises and buildings.

Says Braid: "No matter what our status, we know we built this country. There's this incredible sense of power and self-sufficiency with being in the trades. Our pride comes from knowing we produce value."✦

Question box

1. Would you like to see someone in your family — your son or daughter — apprentice in a trade? How about yourself?

2. Do you think North Americans idealize people who seem wealthy without having to work at it?

22. Is money the cure?

Q: You're smart, hard-working, highly educated. You're a doctor. You make life-and-death decisions about patients. The government wants to cap your income, albeit at a level much higher than almost anyone else in society. Do you oppose it?

✦✦✦✦✦

What would cause a spokesperson for physicians to refer to more than $10,000 a year as "nickels and dimes?" That's how an official representing a major medical association recently tried to play down the extra income a typical physician brings in each year for work billed to secondary sources.

To many wage earners, $10,000 amounts to half a year's salary. But to physicians, it's a small fraction of their earnings, which average roughly $90,000 after expenses for general practitioners and $150,000 after expenses for specialists. Many physicians make much, much more money. Some staunchly argue they deserve their high earnings. But, for good or ill, public-opinion polls shows most North Americans believe physicians practice a greed profession.

All of us have to watch we don't get single-minded about pursuing our own financial success through work. It could lead to narrow lives and broken relationships. But when doctors become obsessed with money, the ramifications are often larger: life and death, health and illness, and the well-being of our communities hang in the balance.

The United States and Canada have many caring, dedicated, thoughtful physicians, but medical ethics specialist David Zimmerman says it's just an historical accident physicians on this side of the Atlantic make unusually high earnings. "North American doctors, as a profession, have emerged as remarkably privileged by comparison with Europe," he says. "American doctors, in particular, love the privilege. Canadian doctors are not quite as extreme, but they're still wedded to it. It distorts how they think about distributive justice, about how individuals should share the benefits and burdens of society."

Governments across North America have been furrowing their brows to find ways to bring down swelling health-care costs. The burden on individuals and communities is becoming unbearable.

The long, unnecessarily brutal training process most physicians have to endure leads to too many succumbing to greed in later years, says Arthur Schafer, head of the Centre for Professional and Applied Ethics. "If we were more human and civilized toward young trainees, they wouldn't be so acquisitive and greedy when they grow older," he says. "I think the fact they have to live in poverty for so many years, have to postpone forming families, have to work such ridiculous hours, which are horrible for them and unsafe for us, almost guarantees when they graduate they will want to get rich quick."

Schafer favors dropping 100-hour-plus work weeks for physicians-in-training and offering them decent hours, working conditions, and salary. In return, the trainees would be asked to "go without the huge pot of wealth once they graduate." It's also important to expose "the myth of physician autonomy," says Schafer, who has consulted for medical societies in the United States and Canada. Physicians are not always the best arbiters of how many days a patient should stay in a hospital, which prescriptions are issued, and whether surgery should take place. It's clear physicians' judgment deserves scrutiny when some American hospitals, for example, deliver 90% of babies through expensive Caesarean sections, while Dutch hospitals deliver only 3% of births by Caesarean, and with a better mortality rate.

To control costs, many physicians have already allowed their procedures to undergo peer review. "What I think is happening is the public, and some doctors, are only beginning to learn the kind of information health economists and health statisticians have known for decades," says Schafer.

Two international leaders in health economics, Professor Robert Evans and Dr. Michael Rachlis, co-authors of *Second Opinion*, have highlighted numerous ways to trim costs. They've suggested everything from limiting the number of practicing physicians to emphasizing preventive, community-based health.

But some physicians don't want to get involved. The former president of the Canadian Medical Association, Dr. John O'Brien-Bell, says it's up to the public — not those "whose role it is to save life" — to make tough ethical choices about how to make health care affordable. That seems an odd view. Everyone has to take part in such an important discussion. The public needs to control panic about running to emergency wards on whims. Rising drug costs have to be monitored. Expensive, high-tech "miracle" procedures need to be probed. And physicians, with their skills, knowledge and high earnings, need to help come up with solutions that will keep the health care system intact.

"We are in a situation of scarcity and to waste resources is in itself an ethical issue," Schafer says. "We need more regulations to ensure health-care expenditures really do benefit patients, and not just the pocketbooks of drug company executives and doctors."

One of the more exciting possibilities some physicians have already begun considering is dropping their fee-for-service system and replacing it with pre-set salaries. "Unfortunately, we have a fee-for-service system which often dictates that physician's self-interest is better promoted by seeing a lot of patients and spending very little time with them," says Schafer. Many physicians argue they need fee-for-service as a financial incentive to do their best work, to follow the Hippocratic oath to put their patients' welfare first. But the fee-for-service incentive collides head on with efforts to be financially responsible. Any market system in which the provider determines demand is not efficient, let alone just, says Zimmerman. Even the most well-meaning physicians are influenced by the fact they'll make more money if they prescribe more, order more tests and do more surgery — and avoid spending time counselling patients.

And physicians may not even be the right person for many people to see. "A patient may need health-care information more than a prescription. It may often be better for them to see public health nurses or social workers." It's almost inevitable, Schafer says, that Canada, and perhaps the United States, will move toward giving physicians salaries. A survey of 2,000 Canadian physicians found 42% approved of a salaried system that included benefits such as pension and overtime payments.

"The fact there are more women in the profession will contribute to this. Women seem less hostile than their male colleagues to salaried work and reasonable working hours. Women very often want to live fuller, better-rounded lives."

In the health-care cost debate, such lifestyle issues point to perhaps the most difficult challenge for physicians, not to mention most of us: to break from society's customary way of measuring personal worth.

"It's the ideology of lawyers, business people, and everybody else virtually," says Schafer. "They measure their success by their level of income."✦

23. *Pass your ambition around*

Q: You're a realtor. You stand to make a big commission from a couple with children who want an expensive house. You know the mortgage will stretch the couple dangerously. Do you encourage them to buy a less expensive house, even though you would get a smaller commission?

◆◆◆◆◆

Oscar Wilde said that ambition is "the last refuge of the failure." According to G.K. Chesterton, "The vulgar man is always the most distinguished, for the very desire to be distinguished is vulgar." And Nancy Astor said that the penalty of success "is to be bored by the people who used to snub you."

What's so funny about ambition? The drive for success that parents try to inculcate in children is turning into a bit of a joke. The "strong desire to achieve something," as the Oxford Dictionary defines ambition, often leads these days to friends' suspicions and even your own dissatisfaction.

No one likes to have to explain jokes. But ethics specialist Mark Wexler thinks humorists have seized on ambition because it's an example of modern irony. "As Oscar Wilde says, the obsessively ambitious person is a failure." Like the infamous type-A personality, he says "a driven, ambitious person seeks power and control because he is insecure. He seeks respect and approval, but he never gets enough. There's always someone who has more. When you meet a person who is ambitious, try ignoring them. It drives them crazy."

Jokes aside, one is hard-pressed to find an affirming quote about ambition in a browse through Bartlett's *Familiar Quotations*. T.S. Eliot linked ambition to vanity, and the late U.S. president John F. Kennedy told Americans world peace would come only if they could look beyond their own ambitions.

Lately, ambition has been questioned even on American television shows — which usually play cheerleader for those in sports, commerce, or patriotism scrambling to holler "We're number one!" Characters on shows from *Thirtysomething* to *Northern Exposure* have searched their souls about whether to work for companies with questionable environmental records. They're climbing the corporate ladder, but wrestling with questions many of us ask ourselves: Does ambition exclude ethics?

Positive ambition does exist, Wexler says. But ambition has received bad press because it's been reduced to mean, self-centered achievement.

"Negative ambition creates a notion of getting ahead by having to push others aside," says Wexler, a business ethicist and editor of *The Journal of Ideology*, who doesn't apologize for branching out freely into philosophy, history, psychology, and religion. "Negative ambition uses other human beings. You get on a capitalist treadmill, like Donald Trump. The reward is upward mobility, but the world around you (such as the environment, family, and community) becomes incidental and peripheral and tends to get hurt. If I elbow you out of the way to get something, how am I doing the world any good?"

The Western idea of ambition has been messed up by an incomplete understanding of the thought of philosopher Adam Smith, the father of laissez-faire capitalism. Smith didn't promote unbridled greed in his classic treatise, *The Wealth of Nations*, Wexler says. Although he envisioned a free market based on individuals pursuing self-betterment, Smith spent most of his time writing about how competitive people are often led by "an invisible hand" that indirectly leads to them advancing the interests of all society.

Critical of corporations and monopolies, Smith believed human conscience would bring self-interest under control so nations would benefit. Smith was also a man of integrity, who anonymously donated huge sums to charity and, unlike modern-day Trumps, believed in limits to growth. He was convinced there is a time to say no to ambition and to stop acquiring things.

Although Wexler thinks Smith's invisible-hand argument is flawed, the ethicist says the famous 17th-century philosopher provided the seeds for a constructive approach to ambition. Smith showed the trick to making ambition positive is balance.

People should be ambitious not only in work, but in all aspects of life: education, growth, commitment, reading, charity, friendship, love. You name it.

"Ambition is an open quest for challenge," Wexler says. We applaud precise surgeons, compelling writers, efficient plumbers, conscientious waiters, sensitive therapists, strong friends, dedicated activists, insightful teachers, and determined, creative business people.

Balanced ambition, unlike obsessive ambition, is to be encouraged in ourselves and our children. It is not the kind of ambition that fears losing. We should enjoy the challenge of soccer, for example, for the game itself, and not necessarily victory. "We can even be aggressive," Wexler says, "but not in a way that shuts others out."

The late Harvard philosopher-mathematician, Alfred North Whitehead, believed all living things, from microscopic cells to human beings, pursue their own enjoyment. Those who follow Whitehead's thinking, called process philosophy, believe an ethical system can be based on the principle of maximizing the enjoyment of all.

Many, however, think enjoyment must be grasped for oneself only. When they have sex, they think only of the pleasure they receive. When they realize their ambition to own a beautiful piece of property, they anxiously keep it just to themselves. "But there's a lot of enjoyment to go around," Wexler says.

Enjoyment is best found through sharing. Life is an interconnected dance. When one dancer experiences enjoyment, so does the partner. That can happen in work. "You will find a great amount of joy," Wexler says, "when two men help a third man put together his barn."✦

Question box

1. What would you like to accomplish?
   What ambitions do you have?

2. Are they ambitions that will hurt others?
   Are they ambitions others may enjoy?

Part 4
Thinking globally

Think globally, but act locally.

Rene Dubos

◆◆◆◆◆

War, the population explosion, environmental decay, pacifism, international trade, civil disobedience, political ethics. Some things seem so overwhelming and beyond us, we'd just like to forget them. But our community doesn't end at the nearest shopping mall. On an increasingly interconnected globe, we need to stay reasonably informed about what's making the world go round — and awry. Democracy, and all the fragile freedoms it preserves, is at stake. As the late U.S. president, Woodrow Wilson, said, long before telecommunications shrank the globe, "We are citizens of the world, and the tragedy of our time is we do not know it."◆

24. *Ecology versus the economy*

Q: You need to get your family out of severe debt.
You are advised to invest in a mining company
that provides jobs in Central America, but suc-
ceeds mainly because of lax environmental regulations. You are sure to profit. Do you invest?

✦✦✦✦✦

Thinning ozone, contaminated drinking water, polluted fish-
spawning streams, styrofoam packaging, blue-box recycling,
factory farming, car exhaust fumes, animals in captivity, lead
paint poisoning, pulp mill pollution, drift-net fishing, sewage
treatment, sick buildings.

Everybody's worried about the globe's future. The environment consistently ranks among citizens' major concerns in
opinion polls, alternating for top spot with the economy. But
often the responsibility we feel for saving the Earth feels as if
it's smothering us. Which eco-battle do we sign up for?
Should we be just looking after human interests, or protecting
animal and plant life for its own sake?

Rather than throw up our hands in despair, it's valuable
to try to get a grip on the big picture in environmental ethics:
the over-arching, can't-be-denied ecological issues, both
pragmatic and philosophical.

Based on a sampling of environmentalists and ethicists, it
turns out it is appropriate that the environment and the
economy vie for the title of North Americans' main worry. In
many ways, the ecology's prime adversary is the economy.

The clash occurs when people act as if the economy is more important than nature. And at some point, who doesn't? When we drive cars to work, flush the toilet, throw out plastic bags, and consume resources, we're involved, to a greater or lesser extent, in abusing the environment.

Ethics specialist Peter Danielson believes the two biggest environmental crises today are global warming and the population explosion. He is not alone. Major environmental organizations also cite global warming and population growth as mammoth concerns; their impact on the health of the planet and its inhabitants threatens to be far-reaching. Few escape.

Ethically, the answer to global warming is simple, says Danielson, who is a director of a committee called The Ethics of Climate Change: Global Warming, which is sponsored by business and government. The committee (and virtually everyone else) believes car exhaust, deforestation, and methane production by agricultural animals, the three causes of global warming, must be curtailed.

But practically, because economies rely heavily on cars, forestry, meat-eating, and ranching, and because restrictions on polluting are so difficult to coordinate among countries, global warming is extremely hard to control. A world population that is increasing at the rate of 250,000 people per day is also difficult to stop, but mainly for social and ethical reasons. It would be relatively simple to bring in child-production quotas, but who should be asked, or forced, to stop procreating?

Environmental planner William Rees says the main reason we're having trouble solving the planet's ecological crisis is because those in power have bought into a world view that says the only thing that counts is economics. "Economic efficiency is the main ethic in our society," says Rees. "We operate on a system called scientific materialism, which says nothing really matters unless it can be measured or quantified. This world view disallows questions of obligation and duty, not only to the environment, but to people."

Within that dominant economic world view, Rees says the single idea most threatening to the environment is globalization of markets. "Global economics is, right off the top, ecologically irrational." Global markets are utterly insensitive to bio-regions, he says. The global profit-taking motive dictates, for example, that fish harvesters should feel no moral qualms if they can make money faster by wiping out a local fish stock and investing elsewhere.

Even though many people think free trade is inevitable, the ideology behind unfettered free trade is bereft of ecological regard, Rees says. When the United States tried to ban the import of canned tuna on the grounds the drift-netting technique was also killing 100,000 dolphins a year, Rees says world trade organizations such as GATT (General Agreement on Tariffs and Trade) said no way. "Mere" distress about the environment must give way to the principle of unrestricted trade.

Philosopher Michael McDonald also sees the ecology caught in a battle of "'sustainability versus competition." The whole idea of environmentally sustainable development, popularized in the United Nations-commissioned Bruntland Report, is an attempt to find a way beyond the "winner-loser" approach to economic development, in which the wealthy and the First World generally gain at the expense of the environment, the poor, the Third World, and future generations.

"We want a society that uses its fair share of resources. But at the same time we also hear strong talk about increasing competitiveness. We're being pushed in both directions. These are very profound forces in contradiction to each other."

Business people often ask McDonald whether it's possible to be both green and competitive. Their challenge now focuses on producing more economic "win-win" situations. Businesses can help themselves and the environment through things such as selling green technology and more efficiently using resources.

But there's a catch. "What happens when it's cheaper and more efficient for a company just to waste stuff?" asks McDonald, who has worked as a consulting ethicist for the Atomic Energy Board of Canada. "What happens when a company wants to extract resources as cheaply as possible and says to a government: 'If you bring in laws that make it more difficult for us, we'll just move to a country that's a lot more friendly to mining or forestry?'" A workable international policy needs to be hammered out that strikes a sustainable balance between nature and finance.

At an elevated philosophical plane, the biggest issue in environmental ethics centers on the value of humans versus the value of animals and plants. But pragmatic environmentalists worry this philosophical debate goes nowhere. It's a luxury we can't afford right now. For the foreseeable future, humans are going to continue to use plants and eat animals. Environmentalists must promote the idea of humans' enlightened self-interest, says Rees. "To save the world, we must appeal to self-interest. If we can demonstrate the survival of human beings depends on the integrity of the ozone layer, halting global CO_2 emissions, and maintaining biological diversity, then people may begin to pay attention."

Environmentalists will continue to be divided between anthropocentrists, who put human self-interest first, and deep ecologists, who hold dear all sentient beings and even organic life. But that doesn't mean environmentalists are hopelessly divided. While it would be nice to come up with a clear cut, unambiguous way to attain environmental sustainability, it's impossible to be pure when real ecological progress must be made soon in a world of sometimes brutal realpolitik. There's enough agreement among environmentalists to push for concerted change.

A mix of human self-interest and respect for all the earth will be needed in any world view capable of taking on looming environmental destruction.✦

Question box

1. Have you been in a situation where it's been easier or cheaper for you to harm the environment, rather than protect it?

2. What do you think are the more important environmental problems in your community? How do they relate to global challenges?

3. Can you think of examples where your self-interest would lead to your protecting the environment?

4. Do you believe all sentient beings (everything capable of thinking and feeling) are worthy of respect and protection?

25. *Defusing the population bomb*

Q: You have two children. You and your spouse have always wanted four. You can afford four. Do you go for it?

◆◆◆◆◆

Endless mountains. Vast prairies. Long coastlines. Beautiful parks. Sometimes nature seems unlimited in North America.

Many cheer when census figures show we've had population increases. With more people, many believe, we'll have a stronger economy. That attitude has led to much of the Western world acting laid back about the number of human bodies on the Earth.

You have to go back to 1968 to find a time when North Americans got worked up about population growth. That's when Stanford University biologist Paul Ehrlich wrote his seminal book, *The Population Bomb*, and a few conscientious couples chose to limit their baby production to two. Since that book came out, however, 1.7 billion more people walk the earth. About 5.5 billion people now inhabit the globe. By 2020, according to the United Nations, there will be more than 10 billion. The numbers are too great to comprehend.

Occasionally, we read about incredible poverty and malnourishment in cities such as Calcutta, Rio de Janeiro, Mexico City, or Jakarta — cities that give new meaning to the term high density. But the problem seems so distant. It turns out, however, Canada and the United States aren't as far removed from the population squeeze as it might appear. An average

North American does 20 to 100 times more damage to the environment than one person from the Third World, say Ehrlich and his wife, Anne, in their recent book, *The Population Explosion*.

Obviously, the First World has to start conserving. But that wouldn't end the population problem. So far, say the Ehrlichs, we've barely managed to feed most of the people on Earth. And we've done it by ruthlessly exploiting arable land, fish stocks, and energy supplies. World grain production is dropping because we've overworked agricultural lands. Every year 95 million more people enter the world, and every year we lose 26 billion tonnes of topsoil (equal to all Australia's wheatlands). Uncontrolled irrigation has also damaged the world's water sources, in some cases permanently. Such trends can't continue.

Many say the enemy of population control is traditional religions that promote fertility. But others say the big opponents of sustainable populations are influential Western economists. "There is still a body of intellectual opinion that sees increasing population as a positive, particularly to spur economic, GNP-measured growth," writes economist-ecologist Hazel Henderson. The author of *Paradigms In Progress: Life Beyond Economics*, notes how a recent cover of *Business Week* magazine asked: "Does America Need More Huddled Masses?" Its answer: Yes.

"These views were much favored by the Reagan administration, supported by religious groups, and led to the U.S. sabotage of many population-stabilization initiatives in the world community during the 1980s," writes Henderson. Most economists fail to take seriously the population threat because they've never been trained to include the ecology in their bottom line.

Economists do not assume the Earth has limits, that resources are finite, say Herman Daly and John Cobb, authors of *For the Common Good: Redirecting the Economy Toward Community, the Environment and a Sustainable Future.* The authors of the award-winning book agree with orthodox economists that the standard of living needs to increase for the poorest two-thirds of the world. But how can the impoverished have more food, TVs, air conditioners, and even swimming pools if their population keeps doubling every 30 years?

A prime reason the wealthy West has grown complacent about the swelling masses is it's bought into the idea that economic growth is itself the answer to over-population. After all, we've seen European and North American countries drop baby production after becoming prosperous. (The birthrate in Canada and the United States is now about 1.8 per couple, below the 2.1 needed to maintain stability. Increased immigration accounts for our growth.)

But populations are just not leveling off in poor countries where factories are opening up. Sadly, newly industrialized nations are often getting stuck in a stage of development characterized by declining death rate, but continuously rising birthrate.

These countries are not making economic and social gains sufficient to reduce births. In some cases, population pressure among the millions toiling in Third World industries is producing famine and pestilence — knocking countries back to where they started: high birthrate, high death rate (the most cruel form of population control).

There is also a potentially sinister reason for economists' open-arms approach to floods of babies, say Daly and Cobb. Unfettered population expansion means cheaper labor — just the way free trade and free migration create greater competition among workers, resulting in lower wages. "The effusive welcoming of unlimited births is often the upper class welcoming the replenishment of the lower class, which supplies useful citizens who are willing to work hard for low wages. What would we do without them!"

Another flaw exists in trusting economic growth to nip the population bud. The theory presupposes a massive redistribution of economic wealth, or a tremendous expansion of the total world economy, so enough wealth would trickle down from the super-rich to the poorest. Neither event is likely to happen.

There are those who believe the First World cannot smugly tell the poor to stop procreating. But 45 heads of state from many of the world's most populated countries — including China, India, Indonesia, Bangladesh, Nigeria, and Egypt — issued a statement in 1987 on population stabilization. It said, in part: "Degradation of the world environment, income inequality, and the potential for conflict exist today because of over-consumption and overpopulation. We believe that the time has come now to recognize the world-wide necessity to stop population growth within the near future."

These leaders said it all. The real question is not whether population should be stabilized, but how?

One of the world's most dramatic efforts to fix the damage wrought by the population explosion began this century in China. China's move to restrict couples to only one child eased grinding poverty in the country of 1.2 billion, which will soon no longer be the earth's most populous nation. But China's coercive birth-control measure not only created troubling side-effects, it raised a challenging ethical issue: How should we balance individual rights against the potential survival of the community?

Interestingly, the American champion of individual rights, John Stuart Mill, argued in his classic book, *On Liberty*, that the state should be able to limit reproductive freedom for the common good. This tension between individualism and community is in the forefront for those convinced the globe cannot maintain an exponentially expanding population, that finite resources are being gobbled up with unsustainable hunger, that the fruitful earth is only so resilient to human exploitation.

Reducing the consumption of rich countries is half of the two-pronged attempt needed to defuse the population bomb. After all, if the average North American baby will consume 50 times more resources than an Indian baby, that means the ecologically relevant population of Canada is about 1.5 billion. This same formula puts the effective population of the United States in the tens of billions. The good news is, in many countries, sustainable populations can probably be attained without China's toughness.

One of the best ways to cut birth rates is to raise women's status. Common wisdom has it that economic expansion automatically lowers women's baby-making urges. Proponents say: Just look at how the baby flow reduced to a trickle after Western countries became economically comfortable.

But many groups, including the United Nations, now say the real force behind declining populations has actually been rising respect for women and support for women's programs. "The drop in fertility which occurred in many countries is more a function of the social, economic, and political liberation of women than of industrialization per se," says Hazel Henderson.

Another non-coercive, inexpensive (and controversial) way to promote low birthrates is to adjust religious values that push women to be fertile. Women should not be pressured, by society or religion, to have big families or unwanted children.

At the time of Jesus, only 200 million people dotted the earth. "In earlier times when more children were an asset to the community as a whole, a woman had an obligation to have many children," says Daly and Cobb in *For the Common Good*. "All the great traditional religions arose during that period, and their teachings are deeply affected by that social need. Today, however, a different attitude is required. Having children is a privilege rather than a duty."

Some of us sneer at women and men who decide not to have children. We think they're self-centered. But those who avoid reproducing deserve respect and appreciation. They're easing the squeeze on a globe that gains 90 million extra people each year. "Childless adults should be aided and morally encouraged to act on their choice," says Dayl, an economist, and Cobb, a philosopher/theologian.

Another way to cut births, without cutting liberties, is to reduce the flood of babies born to teenage girls. In the United States alone, adolescents give birth to more than 500,000 babies a year. The rate is still rising — stimulated by drugs, TV, alcohol, and sex-obsessed entertainment. Many teenage mothers lock into lives of poverty. Taxpayers pay billions to support their families. There aren't easy answers to this teenage crisis. But sex education is badly needed, as is better education for all and greater opportunities that will give young women hope for a brighter future.

Not the type to shirk volatile topics, Daly and Cobb also suggest when all else fails for pregnant teenagers, "abortion is sometimes the least evil of the options." The authors also take on the morally charged subject of euthanasia, saying older people should have the right to die on their own terms. The population threat is one of many reasons to cautiously take humane steps to grant the elderly the right to forgo extraordinary, expensive medical measures long after their lives cease to have any meaning for themselves and others.

While Cobb and Daly don't want to force population-reduction methods on people, they don't rule out restricting individual rights in the interests of the well-being of the Earth, including its people and its dwindling animal species. China's hard-core one-baby law, though beneficial in many respects, apparently had the unwelcome effect of producing "little emperors and empresses." It also created children without brothers and sisters, cousins, uncles, and aunts.

A less coercive approach is called the "transferable birth quota." Developed over decades, it is a flexible baby-limiting system based on market principles. The transferable birth quota basically allows the community to decide how much each couple should reproduce. The population of Canada and the United States would remain roughly stable if every Canadian couple got the equal right to create two babies. And since many do not want to have any children, and others want to have more than two, couples would be able to sell or give away their rights to have children. This would ensure those who want to reproduce beyond the two-baby quota have the desire and ability to pay for it.

The main objection to this plan is that money may determine if a couple has more than two children. But whether we like it or not, financial ability has always influenced whether we have babies and whether they're raised in a healthy way.

The transferable birth quota undoubtedly makes some people squirm. It's not without complications, but it is far less harsh than the Chinese approach. It tries to strike a working trade-off between individual liberty and community need.

Global agreements on such sustainable-population schemes must soon be seriously considered. In the meantime, we should be supporting non-coercive efforts to give women more rights, ending religiously inspired notions that make producing babies a woman's duty, and educating against teenage pregnancy.

About 2,400 babies were born in the time it took the average person to read this chapter on population. The world is shrinking. Fast.✦

1. How do you feel about couples who choose not to have children?

2. What are some ways North Americans are affected by the population explosion?

3. Do you think we can limit individual rights for the sake of the common good?

26. A just war is hard to find

Q: Your government has been overthrown by a violent group. You are asked to join the underground. Do you?

◆◆◆◆◆

In war, an institution dedicated to people killing people, few things seem more distant than ethics. Peace lovers tend to throw their hands up in despair, believing war destroys rules and morals as effectively as a cruise missile wipes out lives, thinking war is never justified.

War supporters also believe values go up in a plume of smoke during war, but tend to respond the opposite way. Winning becomes everything. Virtually any action is permitted so their side prevails.

But there is a middle ground between total pacifism and might-makes-right. Paradoxical as it might seem, there can be an ethics of war. Although rare in history, a just war is possible. The European resistance to Nazi occupation during the World War II ranks as a classic example of a just war.

But World War I, Vietnam, El Salvador, Afghanistan, and many more do not come close to fitting the definition of a just war — a concept struggled over by thinkers ranging from 13th-century theologian Thomas Aquinas to ancient Chinese philosophers and modern social analysts.

The most recent major war that sticks in North Americans' minds is the Gulf War. Applying the ethics of just-war theory to the Middle East encounter, Michael

McDonald argues that the U.S.-led coalition may have met some ethical criteria, but certainly not all. Neither side in that showdown emerged clean.

Trying to be as consistent and rational as one can be about soaring missiles and humans in agony, McDonald, who is head of the Centre for Applied Ethics in Vancouver, says war has three stages: build-up, battle, and aftermath. They are subject to different ethical tests.

In the Gulf War, multinational forces seemed to stand on solid ground on the first ethical test: Was there adequate cause to go to war? Iraqi brutality toward the people of Kuwait, which appeared to have been verified by independent agencies such as Amnesty International, was clearly morally repugnant. But months after the Gulf War ended, investigative journalists revealed that the most highly publicized atrocity by Iraqi troops, the stealing of hospital incubators holding sick Kuwaiti children, was not what it had been billed. Most of it was sheer propaganda coordinated by the Kuwaiti royal family and a public relations company.

On the next test of a just war — whether all peaceful alternatives had been explored — multinational forces fell far short. "Did we really give sanctions enough time to work?" McDonald asks. "I'm not convinced we'd used up reasonable alternatives. I'm not convinced the blockade was a failure." Sanctions had Iraq under extreme pressure, he says, before U.S. President George Bush set a January 15 deadline and attacked.

Although the United States has been criticized for bombarding Iraq because of its valuable oil supplies (critics say there would have been no war if Iraq's chief export was broccoli), McDonald says, "Morality doesn't say you have to give up your own self-interest." The role of ethics in war is to restrain self-interest, he says. However, he notes that citizens of Canada, which has abundant oil reserves, are more than justified in asking whether Ottawa properly served their interests by helping attack Iraq for the sake of securing oil supplies.

The moral purity of the U.S.-led forces is also weakened because they entered battle without a clean slate. Only a few months before the war began, Iraq had been an ally of the United States. In Iraq's eight-year war with Iran's Ayatollah Khomeini, Iraq used U.S.-made weapons, and chemical warfare against the Kurds. The U.S. failed to vigorously oppose the deployment of chemical weapons. The United States has also supported other questionable wars this century, say McDonald and other ethicists. "It's tempting to say one side is bad and the other is good. But both sides, the United States and Iraq, have blood on their hands."

Once battle begins, a different set of ethics, involving "the limits on the use of violence," come into effect. "The most important constraint in battle is the distinction between noncombatants and combatants. Some people are innocent," McDonald says. The chilling reality of 20th-century war is that civilian casualties now fly as high as cruise and scud missiles. With hand-to-hand combat virtually extinct, 50 civilians are now killed for every soldier, say military analysts.

Before the creation of weapons of mass destruction — such as artillery, aerial bombardment, and atomic weapons — military specialists estimated only one civilian died for every soldier. But high-level bombing is indiscriminate. Despite the touted pinpoint accuracy of bombing against Iraq, there is little doubt that U.S.-led forces killed thousands of civilians in Baghdad. Military targets in the Middle East often exist in residential neighborhoods, just as they do in North America. For its part, Iraq did not even pretend to avoid making targets of citizens; it openly bombed Israeli apartment blocks.

Two additional conventions of a just war have been breached by Iraq. In its past war with Iran, Iraq's clouds of poison gas killed anything in their unpredictable path. And like medieval knights who literally used civilians' bodies to protect against arrows and stones, Iraq threatened to place prisoners-of-war at key targets as human shields to frighten off multinational bomb attacks.

Even in a just war, however, soldiers are acceptable targets. One of the ethical tragedies of battle is that fresh-faced youths, often serving involuntarily, can be justifiably killed. "They've taken up arms. The just-war tradition is that you can use force to protect yourself from force."

Finally, the outcome of the Gulf War must also be subject to ethical scrutiny. "If there's such a thing as war passing moral muster, you have to ask the long-range consequences," McDonald says. "You have to ask if the moral gains outweigh the moral losses." That's where he has a lot of trouble with the Gulf War.

Even though the U.S.-led forces blasted their way to victory, there has been bitterness among many of the Middle East's 170-million Muslim Arabs. An occupation by multinational forces would have further exacerbated anti-West hatred. That's why the Kurds suffered after the war at the hands of Saddam Hussein without receiving direct military protection from the allies. "The thinking that you could impose an American peace was not likely. That's really disturbing. There's this image of marching down a road from which there's no retreat."

The West has colonized the Middle East for centuries. "And the Arabs have a very long memory. And we have a kind of short-sighted view." A U.S.-led victory, McDonald says, has added to some Arabs' sense of injustice, and that could easily lead to further wars.

Despite immorality, hypocrisy, and blood on both sides of the Gulf war and other conflagrations, McDonald urges the world's citizens to avoid turning their backs in disgust on tough ethical questions about war. "You can't just say it's such a mess, you can't make a moral judgment." It's important to keep probing at perhaps the ultimate question of war: Is it worth it? Do the lives lost, damage inflicted and long-range negative consequences outweigh the good? "The point," he says, "is not just whether it's worth it for your own country, but for all people affected — including the other side." ✦

Question box

1. Have you ever supported a war?
   Have you opposed wars? Why?

2. Do you think wars can be ethical — especially in an age of high-tech weaponry?

27. *Fighting the power, respectfully*

Q: Your government has allowed logging of one of the last stands of virgin timber in your region. You vehemently oppose the decision. Would you join a peaceful protest, even if it meant arrest?

✦✦✦✦✦

Los Angeles erupted in a violent uprising when a jury acquitted white police officers of beating black motorist Rodney King. Anti-abortionists have fire-bombed abortion clinics; one killed a doctor who performed abortions. Environmentalists have sabotaged logging equipment, and native Indians have armed themselves to protect their land.

With the world appearing to go to hell in a hand basket, choked with poverty, corrupted leaders, suspect courts, and a pulverized environment, public frustration is rising. More and more, citizens' sense of powerlessness is exploding in ugly demonstrations. Some protesters are gaining a surprising amount of public support for picking up guns and tearing down property in the name of their movement.

While many activists may be backing the right cause, they could be doing the wrong thing. It is not easy to pull off an ethical protest.

Yet Alan Borovoy, chief legal counsel for the Canadian Civil Liberties Association, has consistently done so. So have Jim and Shelley Douglass, heads of the U.S. anti-nuclear campaign, who believe sometimes activists are compelled to break the law. Politely.

In his 57 years, Borovoy has disrupted hundreds of class-rooms to oppose mandatory religious instruction in public schools, shut down a major city's library system to protest anti-pornography laws, and marched on upset whites to improve conditions on Native reserves. Flamboyant and garrulous, Borovoy admits to getting a kick out of pricking authority.

The thing is, Borovoy's protests have always been non-violent. Just as important for him, they've always been legal. In the United States and Canada, he thinks all protests should be both.

That's why he's disturbed that millions of people appear to support violent protests. In just one example, when the Mohawk Indians in Quebec took up arms to stop land they considered sacred from being turned into a golf course, commentators said the Indians "had no other option." The title of Borovoy's book, *Uncivil Obedience: The Tactics and Tales of a Democratic Agitator,* points to how Borovoy believes there are nearly always effective, legal options to bring about social change.

"You can goad, disrupt, pressure, hurt, and discomfort, without breaking the law," he says. Political embarrassment, strikes, institutional shutdowns, and satire go a long way toward that. "It's possible to be completely obedient to the law and absolutely miserable to the government at the same time." One of many options Borovoy suggests the Mohawks could have tried included organizing a boycott of stores in the nearby town of Oka, whose council sparked the summer-long standoff by trying to push through a golf course on land natives contested.

The only instances where Borovoy has no moral qualms about protesters breaking the law is in undemocratic, totalitarian societies. Law-breaking is also justified, he says, in the situations Martin Luther King found himself in, where southern blacks did not enjoy the same rights as whites in an otherwise democratic country.

Borovoy thinks law-breaking (as well as violence) is contagious, especially in an age of the mass media. The disenfranchised, outraged, and powerless begin believing that flouting the law is the only way to bring about justice. That can create chaos. "The right to assembly is one major democratic freedom protesters rely on," Borovoy says. "It's in the interest of those who seek change to keep democratic processes viable." To quell civil threats, Borovoy fears governments move quickly to wipe out freedoms. "Order is going to prevail in one way or another. And consensus and clout are the two ways of getting it. As consensus erodes, there is a risk it will be replaced by clout."

However, two of North America's most prominent peace activists, the Douglasses, think civil disobedience — illegal protest — is an important ethical option, even in a democracy. "The question is, Which laws are we to respect?" says Jim Douglass, who has spent a total of 18 months in jail for acts of civil disobedience. Civil disobedience should be used cautiously. "Our philosophy is to respect laws, except at those points where the law itself is in deep violation of a larger law" he says. Although Douglass and his followers broke federal law by sitting on the tracks in front of the U.S. government's White Train, which was carrying nuclear weapons to a submarine base in Washington State, Douglass says the demonstrations actually upheld the highest principles of the Geneva Convention.

When the Douglasses take part in civil disobedience, they believe they are upholding, first and foremost, the prime law of virtually all religions: Thou shalt not kill. And the Geneva Convention, which bans killing civilians as well as using "indiscriminate weapons of destruction," is upheld by the U.S. Constitution, Douglass says. There are few weapons more indiscriminate than nuclear arms. In civil disobedience, it is necessary to painstakingly adhere to Gandhi's principles of non-violence, called satyagraha or "truth-force," says Douglass, who, with Shelley, founded the Ground Zero

Center for Non-Violent Action in the U.S. He was interviewed by telephone from his home in a poor black neighborhood in Birmingham, Alabama, where he and Shelley moved in 1989 to follow the White Train.

Jim is also author of the book, *The Non-Violent Coming of God*, which develops the thesis that Jesus was trying to bring in the non-violent "kingdom of God" to stop the destruction of Jerusalem by Roman occupying forces. Jesus, he says, believed force is never permitted in ethical protest. The principles behind civil disobedience are respect for all people and love for one's enemies. "Civil disobedience is never to be used to coerce anyone." Even though White Train protesters symbolized their opposition to nuclear war by welcoming arrest, Douglass says the aim of civil disobedience is to take a stand that will appeal to peoples' consciences. "Our purpose is not to stop the trains. Our purpose is to change the attitude of the people responsible for the trains ... By our willingness to go to jail, and bear some suffering, we make our appeal."

Because of his philosophy, Douglass opposes taking up arms or blocking women from entering abortion clinics. Opponents of the White Train (which he says carried nuclear explosives six times more powerful than all the bombs used in World War II) contacted train engineers months in advance of protests. They never called opponents names. They took great pains to meet with military personnel and their families.

The principle of satyagraha fell apart on one occasion in the mid-1980s, however. A small number of zealous protesters rushed the White Train, creating a panic and almost pushing police in front of the moving locomotive. A lack of respect was shown that day for law enforcement officials and opponents. In that case, Douglass agrees with Borovoy that democracy was threatened.

In fact, despite disagreeing over the validity of breaking the law through civil disobedience, Borovoy and the

Douglasses take similar approaches to ethical protest. They oppose violence, and they urge those seeking justice to use imaginative tactics rather than force.

They suggest creating coalitions, nurturing spiritual strength, and keeping an eye on the long term. The ultimate object of protest is to win hearts and minds, they say. That means replacing aggression with peace, anger with empassioned reason, sloppy outbursts with rigorous planning.

As Gandhi said, there is no point in dying for a cause in an unorganized way.✦

Question box

1. Do you think protesting does any good?

2. Are there any laws you have wanted to break to make a point?

3. What makes a protest effective?

28. Global economics: free or fair?

Q: You will be able to buy some things cheaper if free trade is brought in with a nearby country. But the free-trade accord will mean the end of many jobs, including your neighbor's. Do you support the deal?

◆◆◆◆◆

Global economic competition throws issues at us that are just as challenging as war and the environment. And just as military leaders aren't well known for welcoming opinions from outsiders, neither are economists nor corporate executives.

Fortunately, the public, religious leaders, and scholars are not willing to hand so-called experts total control of our children's economic future. From neighborhood consumer groups boycotting products to liberation theologians who commit to the poor, people all over believe it's worth fighting for something more than the proverbial bottom line: an ethical economy.

It appears many economists are also beginning to question themselves. When professors of economics at 50 major universities were recently asked the question: "Is there a sense of lost moorings in economics?" more than two-thirds answered yes. Pollster Shlomo Maital concluded the discipline of economics is in crisis and a paradigm shift is on its way.

Most economists now promote free trade, but it's coming under increasing suspicion. Public opinion polls show the majority of people in both Canada and the United States believe it can hurt their countries. With a Canada-U.S.-Mexico free trade deal now in effect, labor and environmental groups are among those saying it will lead to lost jobs and ecological destruction.

The seminal book, *For the Common Good: Redirecting the Economy Toward Community, the Environment, and a Sustainable Future,* says current economic policies are leading the globe to environmental and social catastrophe. *For the Common Good* charges many economists with practicing "disciplinolatry" — following an overly abstract and narrow approach to their discipline that blocks out the needs of society. Free trade emerges as one of the prime examples of modern economic theories gone wrong; maximum free trade leads to the destruction of community and ecology.

The book, by John Cobb and Herman Daly, suggests an alternative to free trade: "An economic model that gives moral priority to a national and regional community, and includes both future generations and non-human communities." They point out that the influential economist John Maynard Keynes, who once supported the unrestricted transfer of goods and capital across international boundaries, changed his position in the 1930s.

Keynes stated: "I sympathize with those who minimize, rather than with those who would maximize, economic entanglement between nations. Ideas, knowledge, art, hospitality, travel — these are the things which should of their nature be international. But let goods be homespun whenever it is reasonably and conveniently possible; and, above all, let finance be primarily national."

Keynes' opposition to free trade generally held sway among North America economists until the past couple of decades. Here are some ethical concerns about free trade:

- Free trade promotes growth in freedom and wealth as ultimate values. But it de-emphasizes responsibility to community and assumes, incorrectly, that the environment can sustain limitless growth.

- Communities should generally aim for self-sufficiency. The higher costs of some goods produced in a self-sufficient society, Keynes said, are outweighed by the advantages of local control and enhanced community.

- Allowing corporations, with no guideline other than profit-making, to operate without concern for borders leads to them having virtually no obligation to local communities or countries.

- Under free trade, corporations hop from country to country to take advantage of cheap labor, thereby disrupting communities, leaving behind unemployed, and putting pressure on all workers to lower wages.

- Under free trade, corporations go where there are fewer environmental regulations. Effective international laws are needed, but do not currently exist.

- While proponents say freer trade will lead to greater global GNP, they hide that free trade also leads to greater concentration of capital in fewer hands, with many poor not benefiting.

- Free trade might encourage GNP, but it destroys previously unpaid subsistence economies that prevented much of the now-endemic poverty throughout the world.

- As free trade breaks down community, it leads to humans finding their identity and status as consumers. Shopping has become the great national pastime.

The ultimate goal of an economic system should be to serve neither the collective, nor the individual, say Cobb and Daly, but "persons-in-community."

It should go without saying that most of these viewpoints are not embraced by most free-market economists. Michael Walker, of the conservative lobby group, The Fraser Institute, says people who attack free trade "are almost enough to make you grind your teeth."

Those who oppose free trade run the danger of fostering totalitarianism and a society in which governments "tell people what's best for them," says Walker. He defends free trade by saying it gives consumers what they want (low prices), encourages people around the globe "to be interdependent in an impersonal kind of way" and offers poor countries such as Mexico access to international capital. Worldwide regulations covering the environment, trade, and working conditions would only impoverish people, Walker says. Self-sustainability is another weak concept, he says. North American natives had self-sustaining economies, but endured short, sometimes miserable lives before white man's arrival. "Is that the kind of life we want?" The absolutely free global market operates "in a most marvelous way," Walker says. He quotes the famous argument by 18th-century British economist Adam Smith, who said the self-interested capitalist is guided "as if by an invisible hand" which makes his competitiveness serve all of society, without him even intending it.

However, *For the Common Good* suggests contemporary economists have missed a crucial aspect of Smith's classic theory. It says Smith believed in the "invisible hand" because, as a typical good British citizen, he believed all capitalists would find it in their interest to serve their country first. Smith did not envision a world in which "trans-national corporations transcended governments and no longer see nations as their context."

The authors of *For the Common Good* worry that people of good will do not realize current economic policies are leading to a dead end. They ask economists to heed "the cry of anguish" of the earth and its inhabitants and say an economics of the common good is what those who care about the globe must call for.✦

Question box

1. Do you think free trade will generally improve your life and those of your loved ones? Or do you think it will do more harm?

2. Do you think it's inevitable that global competition will control your local economies?
   Do you think that's okay?

3. What do you think should be the ultimate goal of an economic system?

29. Probing politicians

Q: Two candidates are running for office. One clearly maps out policies and will stick to them through thick and thin. The other is pragmatic, emphasizing a willingness to compromise. Which candidate would you tend to favor?

✦✦✦✦✦

Breach of trust, misuse of public funds, kickbacks, patronage, conflict of interest, waste, and out-and-out theft. It seems a month doesn't go by without some elected official ending up in court, or resigning in disgrace.

The ethics of politicians is hot news all over North America. It's a good thing, too. Here are five reasons political ethics should remain on the front pages:

- Many people believe politicians are the only ones who can hold society together.

  The church now has only "persuasive" powers to influence things such as abortion, the distribution of wealth, and defense policy (in contrast to eras when church and state marched in lock-step). Today's politicians can legislate on life-and-death issues others can only talk about. Politicians also have closer ties to big organizations, such as forestry companies, unions, environmental groups, farmers, doctors associations, and ski-industry lobbyists. Big organizations are replacing the grass-roots. Politics is where the power is. People now look to politicians to express their deepest moral values.

- Political parties are increasingly attracting people who cannot distinguish between serving their own good and the public good.

"Many people are attracted to politics with a very free-enterprise notion. They have a zeal that greed is the best way to go," says Wexler, who has taught business ethics at universities across North America. Some political parties see themselves as the voice of business. "The question then arises: 'Are they representing the public or people with vested interests?'"

When politicians claim running government is just like running a business, Professor Paul Russell says, "the distinction becomes blurred between acting in the public interest and acting for a private business." Although business people can play a valuable role in office, Russell, who has taught at Harvard University, says they're also more likely to have a financial stake in government policy.

- Politicians are becoming reluctant to take clear-cut stands.

In a post-modern world, the idealogies that used to divide up the population are not so neat. For example, the traditional battle between regulated and unregulated markets (left versus right) is breaking down, says Mark Wexler. There is no longer a great difference in the West between governments run by democratic socialists and free enterprisers. Both endorse mixed economies, where the marketplace rolls on while the state takes care of things such as welfare and occasionally uses taxes to stimulate economic growth.

Abortion, transit, capital punishment, education, and ecology also do not sort easily into left-right politics. "You'll find some conservative old gardener who's into ecology up to the hilt. And he's very confused when a conservative party is not into ecology," says Wexler. To deal with a fragmented public, politicians in North America are now likely to package themselves as images.

Instead of categorically declaring their stand on issues, thereby taking an ethical position, politicians emphasize their adaptability and flexibility. "Politics today means you could start out as a liberal and do the same thing as the conservatives would have," says Wexler. On the other hand, conservatives who want small government often run up huge deficits. With such political elasticity, Wexler says "ethics can get blown all to hell."

The trade off for this moral muddiness is efficiency. "If you're interested in growth and prosperity, pragmatic politics is very good," Wexler says. "Things will get done. Business will be served. The trains will run on time."

- In an age of moral confusion, ethics is becoming the focus of intense concern in many walks of life, not only politics.

"You can no longer take for granted a common belief in Judeo-Christian principles," says Paul Russell. We are in an age characterized by pluralism and fragmentation. Medical, business, environmental, and journalistic ethics are increasingly being discussed in schools and society. "People are searching for a common value system. And they get it by discussing ethics in public."

- Having handed politicians great power, the public feels uncomfortable with them acting as moral arbiters.

A suspicious public and media feel politicians must be constantly probed regarding their integrity. Trust is paramount. Citizens want to know: Is that the authentic Ronald Reagan, Brian Mulroney, Jean Chretien, or Bill Clinton?

Although it would be dangerous to expect our politicians to act as saintly as an outstanding religious leader, we win when political ethics is a top issue. It's worth constantly testing whether politicians are ready to put the public's interest first. The system depends on the moral reliability of the people in office.✦

Question box

1. Do you vote for politicians based on their policies or their character?

2. What do you expect of your politicians? Could it be too much?

3. What are the different goals of business and government? Do they clash?

30. Embracing democracy

Q: You don't like any of the candidates in an upcoming election. Do you vote?

✦✦✦✦✦

Democracy seems to be on a roll. From Eastern Europe to the Philippines, the ideal that governments should be run by the people, for the people, is gaining hold in regions where rulers once held sledgehammer authority.

Lord Acton's famous maxim — "Power tends to corrupt and absolute power corrupts absolutely" — has goaded democracy-lovers to challenge authority from Poland to Haiti, Ottawa to Washington. Worldwide reform is reminding people, even in the so-called free world, that those who wield power must never be allowed to take it for granted.

What makes a good democracy? Its touchstone is how much it allows a group of people to determine its own future, says Professor Frank Cunningham, a world-renowned specialist on democratic theory. Democracy efficiently balances competing interests in society, Cunningham says. "But democracy is always precarious. And there's almost never enough of it. Democracy is not a magical state. We always have to struggle to maintain it."

There are two basic types of democracy, Cunningham says: thin and robust. While much of the world still cowers under dictators of the left and right, Cunningham says recently many countries have at least become thin democracies. Thin democracies have the barest democratic essentials: a multi-party system and uncoerced elections. If nothing else, Cunningham says thin democracies have mechanisms "for getting the buggers out." Although Cunningham believes federal, state and provincial, and civic governments in the United States and Canada generally qualify as thin democracies, they sometimes fall short of even that status.

As for robust democracy: it is far more rare than it should be, says Cunningham, who has served as the head of the philosophy department at the University of Toronto. Robust democracy requires "transparent" government decision making, great responsiveness to the public, and a highly educated populace.

How does the government in your region rank as a democracy?

A prime prerequisite of thin democracy is that election results fairly reflect the wishes of the populace. In North America, many elections have been skewed by grossly imbalanced ridings and controversies over boundary tamperings.

Another requirement for thin democracy is politicians who are free of conflict of interest. The public must be confident that politicians are not entering office to pursue their own interests or those of their friends. Politicians must not be making secret deals with developers, forest companies, union leaders, stock promoters, or anyone else with undue influence. "Politicians must be carrying out the wishes of the public. People have to know politicians haven't been bought," says Cunningham. Tough conflict-of-interest laws are required.

The standards of robust democracy are much higher. Government decision making in a robust democracy must be as transparent as possible. "People should be able to have ready and affordable access to what's going on in government. The burden should always lie with those who want to limit the right to know." There should be mandatory disclosure of campaign donations to monitor whether specialist interests, such as businesses or labor groups, are receiving favors for making financial donations. Bold freedom of information acts are also necessary.

An educated, informed, and involved public is also essential to robust democracy. "People," he says, "have to know how to interrogate those in power." To watchdog government, Cunningham says people must have sophisticated training to know how society functions, when they are being manipulated by those in power, and to probe the technical complexities of important issues, such as pollution.

Finally, there is length of time in power. Although longevity is not anti-democratic by definition, uninterrupted reigns increase the chances for abusing power. A party that rules for decades becomes more prone to corruption, laziness, isolation, and favoring insiders. Politicians and senior bureaucrats begin to wield incredible might behind closed doors. An old boys' network develops, and people get jobs not because they're good at what they do, but because they're doing somebody a favor. Extended years of domination can create an arrogance among politicians. They develop an attitude that says, "We're always going to be here. And you'll always have to deal with us."

Political scientist Norman Ruff says most regions — particularly Mexico, which has had the same party in power for much of the century as the result of suspect elections — would have healthier democracies with more frequent "circulation of elites." Major sectors of the populace can become permanently disenfranchised if they're not represented in office. The opposition can grow weak, dominated by unrealistic expectations. "And if one side loses all the time, and loses on something fundamental, moral concerns start to arise. It leads to hostility. It leads to suspicion about the entire democratic process," says Ruff.

The frightening irony of anti-democratic governments everywhere is they can make the public defeatist and passive.

That's how Cunningham says bad governments dig themselves in further. The people stop fighting for democracy.✦

Question box

1. Has anything happened to make you think nearly all politicians are useless?

2. Does the government in your region rank as a thin or robust democracy?

3. Do you think there are better ways to run a world than democracy? What is the ultimate goal of democracy?

Epilogue
Principles to build on

It is very hard to be simple enough to be good.

Ralph Waldo Emerson

Would you read your troubled teenager's diary without permission? Cheat on an exam? Tell your best friend you saw her husband kiss another woman? Give to a panhandler? Join an illegal protest? The questions go on and on.

The people behind a radio game show, called *Choices*, that asked panelists and a studio audience what they'd do in everyday ethical dilemmas emphasized that the questions they asked didn't have right and wrong answers.

Self-revealing discussion was encouraged on the public-radio show, which took the same guilt-free attitude as the popular board game, Scruples, as well as most mass-market magazine quizzes. *Choices* reinforced the idea that ethics is just a matter of personal opinion. Thus, it raised a crucial philosophical issue this book must also deal with directly: Are there universal ethical principles everyone should follow?

The producer who came up with the idea for *Choices* offered her blunt answer: "There is no right or wrong." Moral absolutes do not exist, said the producer. "I hate situations that are black and white."

Society's morals change, the producer said: Being gay was unacceptable 30 years ago, now it's acceptable, more or less, in North America. "The game is called *Choices*, because people

---

choose what's right and wrong," the producer said. "People make the decision that's right for themselves."

The vivacious host, who moved through the studio audience like a deft Donahue, initially said there's "absolutely" no such thing as right or wrong. Pressed further, however, she realized she did think it's wrong to abuse children. "Lines have to be drawn," she said. "I guess to say there is no right or wrong would be an overstatement."

Philosophy professor Arthur Schafer says his first-year ethics students also believe, at first, they're moral relativists. When Schafer asks his class whether there can be an "absolute morality" applicable to all, 90% say no. They believe right and wrong changes with each individual, each culture, each era.

Does that mean slavery was right in the southern United States in the 19th-century? Schafer then asks the students he's taught on campuses from Canada to England's prestigious Oxford University.

Does that mean only whites should vote in South Africa?

Does that mean it was okay for the Nazis to attempt genocide of Jews?

"That's when the students start to backtrack. They begin realizing they don't think anything goes. They don't think something is all right if a majority agrees to it," says Schafer. "Why do so many people feel they're relativists when really they're not? Why do so many people want to reject absolutism?"

Unlike many conservatives, or followers of a religion, secular liberals are often nervous about declaring moral absolutes. It's easy to appreciate people such as *Choices'* producer, who wanted her radio show to promote tolerance because it's "dangerous to impose your moral code on someone else." Liberals often take a relativist position because they realize the pitfalls of self-righteousness. Liberals are sensitive to the damage wrought when one culture sets out to civilize another. Liberals realize people often put down people just because they follow different customs or rituals.

With a telling example of ethnocentrism, Schafer says it's too easy for shocked whites to condemn the Arctic Inuit for killing the old and feeble in their tribes. But the long-gone Inuit practice served to minimize human suffering in a brutally harsh, subsistence culture. Although it would be swinish for well-off whites to kill their super-annuated parents, Schafer says the Inuit custom made it so those who had lived out their lives could die and the whole tribe, particularly the young, would have a chance to survive. Different circumstances, he says, determine which acts are ethical in each culture and time. But many liberals make a mistake when they think changing circumstances removes the need for universal ethical principles that apply across the board.

Two of *Choices'* panelists did believe in universal values. When Bill Richardson, a comedian and radio-show host, was asked if there's such a thing as right and wrong, he paused for a long time, and tentatively said, "Yeeeeeesssssss," as if giving himself the chance to change his mind part way through the answer. Although Richardson saw himself as the show's Everyman, who doesn't do a lot of ethical agonizing, he is probably one of the few mainstream broadcasters to risk coming out about being gay. He's taken a stand. He believes in truth and that people should avoid harming others.

Philosophers say ethics are more than one person's opinion against another. Some values are better than others. Although it won't make ethics a cinch in every sticky situation, three universal guidelines exist that apply to us all:

- We should minimize human suffering. It's bad for humans to suffer needlessly, it's good for humans to flourish.

- Society's benefits and burdens should be distributed justly.

- Treat others as you would like to be treated.

A life of integrity doesn't have to be complicated. It just requires balancing talk about our rights with talk about responsibilities — to our families, communities, colleagues, democracy, and the troubled planet.

It means realizing, since we're all interconnected, we need to try to act for the common good.

It means, to put it simply, being neighborly.✦

OTHER TITLES IN THE SELF-COUNSEL SERIES

GIVING THANKS
Graces for every occasion
by Harvey Haber and Wayne Allen

With this book by your side, you'll be able to add inspiration to any special occasion.

Authors Harvey Haber and Wayne Allen offer 50 inspirational graces that are sure to add the perfect touch to weddings, business conferences, and family dinners. There are graces to ask for divine guidance and words to make us strong enough to set a good example for others. Anyone who becomes tongue-tied or at a loss for words at the mere thought of having to say grace will appreciate these eloquent and heartfelt words of thanks.

This beautifully designed book puts words right at your fingertips. Gently run your finger down the spine and the page will stay open on the grace you desire.

Giving Thanks will be a treasure for people who want to add spiritual nourishment to any meal, holiday, family gathering, or any time a few meaningful words are needed to help set a special tone. $12.95

Features:

- Provides 50 original graces for every type of gathering

- Offers special graces for special occasions

- Features stay-flat Otabind binding

- Attractively designed

FAMILY TIES THAT BIND
A self-help guide to change through
Family of Origin therapy
by Dr. Ronald W. Richardson

Create a better life for yourself. Most people's lives are complicated by family relationships. Birth order, our parents' relationship, and the "rules" we were brought up with can affect our own self-esteem and future relationships with spouses, children, and other family members. Now the Family of Origin theory and techniques recently developed and successfully used by family therapists can help you find different and better ways of dealing with family relationships. This easy-to-read, practical book explains how families function and what you can do to change the way you act in your family and with other important people. Step-by-step exercises show how to apply the principles to your own situation and develop a more positive approach to all aspects of your life. $8.95

Contents include:

- How families work

- You never talk to me — closeness and distance among family members

- You're not better, just different — dealing with differences

- How to be true to yourself and still have friends

- Triangles in relationships

- Who's on first? — Birth order and gender position in the family of origin

- Doing the work — The steps in doing family of origin work

BIRTH ORDER AND YOU
How your sex and position in the family affects your personality and relationships
by Dr. Ron Richardson and Lois A. Richardson, M.A.

Are you the oldest, middle, or youngest child in your family? Are you a leader or a follower? An introvert or an extrovert? Your position in the family has a far-reaching effect on the way you experience the world — it is a cornerstone of your personality. With insight and accuracy, this book shows you the way to a greater understanding of your friends, family, and yourself. $7.95

Some of the topics covered are:

- Why birth order matters

- How the sex of your siblings affects your personality

- Introducing birth order position and sex

- Oldest children

- Youngest children

- Middle children

- Only children

- Twins

- Exceptions and variations: Factors that alter the usual birth order pattern

- Parenting your children of different birth orders

- Siblings as a psychological resource

ORDER FORM

All prices are subject to change without notice. Books are available in book, department, and stationery stores. If you cannot buy the book through a store, please use this order form. (Please print)

Name _____

Address _____

_____

Charge to: ❑Visa ❑ MasterCard

Account Number _____

Validation Date _____

Expiry Date_____

Signature_____

❑**Check here for a free catalogue.**

IN CANADA
Please send your order to the nearest location:
Self-Counsel Press
1481 Charlotte Road
North Vancouver, B. C.
V7J 1H1
Self-Counsel Press
8-2283 Argentia Road
Mississauga, Ontario
L5N 5Z2
IN THE U.S.A.
Please send your order to:
Self-Counsel Press Inc.
1704 N. State Street
Bellingham, WA 98225

YES, please send me:

_____copies of **Giving Thanks**, $12.95

_____copies of **Family Ties That Bind**, $8.95

_____copies of **Birth Order and You**, $7.95

Please add $2.50 for postage & handling.
Canadian residents, please add 7% GST to your order.
WA residents, please add 7.8% sales tax.